PRAISE FOR

AMERICA, A REDEMPTION STORY

"America needs leaders like Tim Scott. The best leaders are those who lead from the heart and through their own example, and Scott does both. Scott is not just a colleague but someone I'm proud to count as a close friend. While I already knew some of his personal story, I was enthralled by the way this memoir blends events from Scott's life with his meditations on our shared history as a nation and his hopes for what we can still become. From the hardship of Scott's growing up years to his leadership on the national stage, *America, a Redemption Story* is a heartfelt page-turner with a vital message: you *can* create positive change if you have the courage to grab hold of the opportunities this great nation provides. I hope everyone in America picks up a copy of this book."

—KEVIN McCARTHY, CONGRESSMAN AND HOUSE MINORITY LEADER

"Tim Scott is a man of faith, fortitude, and boundless hope in the promise of America. Rising from humble beginnings to become one of our nation's foremost champions for freedom and opportunity, Tim's story of resilience and resolve should inspire every American. Through public service and now through the pages of this book, Tim gives us a candid look into his own remarkable life and the lives of fellow Americans who overcame extraordinary odds—pointing us to our highest ideals and the enduring promise of the American Dream while reminding us that each of us has a role to play in writing the next pages of the great American story."

—MIKE PENCE, FORMER VICE PRESIDENT OF THE
UNITED STATES, GOVERNOR, AND CONGRESSMAN

"It's a rare book that not only moves your soul but changes the way you think. Tim Scott's memoir is more than the story of his life—it's also the story of our nation and an impassioned call to every American to seek unity beyond our disagreements and discover new hope in the values we share. The American Dream remains alive and well, and leaders like Tim ensure that our dreams of unity and greatness remain within reach. I've been challenged and encouraged by Tim's book, and I believe it'll do the same for you."

—JOHN MAXWELL, #1 NEW YORK TIMES BESTSELLING
AUTHOR, ENTREPRENEUR, AND LEADERSHIP EXPERT

"Tim Scott has lived the American Dream. He's overcome challenges with faith and prayer, determination and hard work, and God-given courage and imagination. Tim's life is a testament to the greatness of our country, and we are all better off because of his leadership."

—NIKKI HALEY, FORMER AMBASSADOR TO THE UNITED
NATIONS AND FORMER GOVERNOR OF SOUTH CAROLINA

"I've known Senator Scott for years and though we don't see eye to eye on every political nuance, I've found him to be an intelligent, insightful person of great faith. Like a soldier, he has held his post and served his country. His compelling journey from the fringes to the frontlines, reminds us that our diversity is as essential as the contrasted flag that's emblematic to the possibility of a more perfect union. To be sure, we are not there yet. However, this book, *America, a Redemption Story*, encourages debate, discussion, and even disappointment without desecrating the fragility of democracy! There has never been a time where our ideals have been more contrasted by our actions. And yet he reminds us that where we start need not be where we end. I hope you'll read it and see that we must wrestle for reasoned paths to better!"

—BISHOP T. D. JAKES, BISHOP OF THE POTTER'S
HOUSE, AUTHOR, AND FILMMAKER

"Tim Scott's story is bold, inspiring, and empowering. It reminds us of a truth we must never forget: America, despite its failures and imperfections, is a land of profound hope and opportunity. In a season of division and uncertainty, Senator Scott is a beacon of hope whose story encourages every American to hold onto the things that unite us and strive together for a better tomorrow."

—HAROLD FORD JR., FORMER CONGRESSMAN
AND COHOST OF THE FIVE

"Tim Scott made history. But it is his own personal history that is so compelling. His family literally went from picking cotton to picking out a seat in Congress. How it happened will leave you inspired, challenged, and recommitted to the dream that is America."

—TREY GOWDY, FORMER PROSECUTOR AND CONGRESSMAN
AND HOST OF *SUNDAY NIGHT IN AMERICA*

"Tim Scott is an incredible leader with an amazing story. It's been my privilege to take the journey with him for the last twenty-five years as a pastor and friend. His story is an American story. It has both hardship and hope, and it inspires us to believe that there is such a thing as common ideals that produce a greater good. It's a story of hope, faith, family, and possibility. Micah 6:8 says that it is the responsibility of each of us to 'act justly, love mercy and walk humbly with our God.' I have watched Senator Scott live it out and inspire others to do so as well."

—GREG SURRATT, FOUNDER OF SEACOAST CHURCH AND
PRESIDENT OF THE ASSOCIATION OF RELATED CHURCHES

"My great friend Tim Scott has written a book that I hope gets into the hands (and hearts) of every American. Politics can be tough, and Tim has never shied away from a fight if he knew it was worth fighting. But in this extraordinary memoir, Tim sets aside political arguments in favor of storytelling—and what a compelling story it is. Tim's unshakeable hope and his passion for creating opportunities for the people he serves are rooted in his story. He's traveled the path from poverty to success, from feeling lost to finding his purpose. His story, along with the many stories he shares of other Americans who sacrificed much—and accomplished even more—is both an inspiration and a challenge: Will you have the courage to take hold of the opportunities in front of you? Will you become an everyday hero through simple acts of kindness and service? I heartily recommend this book to everyone who shares Tim's hope for a better tomorrow and his commitment to protecting and nurturing America's status as the land of opportunity."

—JOHN RATCLIFFE, ATTORNEY, FORMER MAYOR, CONGRESSMAN,
AND DIRECTOR OF NATIONAL INTELLIGENCE

"In his new book, Senator Tim Scott writes, 'Every American starts his or her journey at vastly different places. The sky is not the limit for all of us.' Tim's journey has been a very hard one. Growing up as a young black man in a poor, single-parent household, Tim had the deck stacked against him. But he found powerful examples and support in his mother, his grandparents, and other mentors God placed in his life. Against all odds, and with God's help, Tim climbed out of his circumstances and became a distinguished and greatly respected United States senator. Tim's faith, courage, and determination will be an inspiration to all who read this book. The more I have gotten to know him and his story, the more impressed I am. His is an American story. You will be encouraged on your journey forward through this book."

—GREG LAURIE, SENIOR PASTOR OF
HARVEST CHRISTIAN FELLOWSHIP

"*America, a Redemption Story* comes from the author's true character and beliefs. My friend Tim Scott chronicles his life in the midst of personal challenges and national crisis. And his journey—from a child growing up in a family in crisis, to a United States senator respected and renowned for his commitment to promoting unity and cooperation as this nation's hope—gives tremendous credibility to his belief that equal access to opportunity is the truest definition of the American Dream. In Tim's own words, 'I have come to believe most, if not all, people are doing the best they can with what they have been given.' May we all be inspired to see the best in each other and build together toward greater understanding and unity."

—BOB JOHNSON, FOUNDER OF BLACK ENTERTAINMENT
TELEVISION AND THE RLJ COMPANIES

AMERICA,
A REDEMPTION STORY

AMERICA,
A REDEMPTION STORY

CHOOSING HOPE, CREATING UNITY

TIM SCOTT
WITH JOEL N. CLARK

NELSON
BOOKS
An Imprint of Thomas Nelson

America, a Redemption Story

Published in Nashville, Tennessee, by Nelson Books, an imprint of Thomas Nelson. Nelson Books and Thomas Nelson are registered trademarks of HarperCollins Christian Publishing, Inc.

Author is represented by the literary agency of The Fedd Agency, Inc., PO Box 341973, Austin, Texas 78734.

Thomas Nelson titles may be purchased in bulk for educational, business, fundraising, or sales promotional use. For information, please email SpecialMarkets@ThomasNelson.com.

Scripture quotations are taken from The Holy Bible, New International Version®, niv®. Copyright © 1973, 1978, 1984, 2011 by Biblica, Inc.® Used by permission of Zondervan. All rights reserved worldwide. www.Zondervan.com. The "NIV" and "New International Version" are trademarks registered in the United States Patent and Trademark Office by Biblica, Inc.®

Unless otherwise noted, photos are taken from the author's personal collection.

Library of Congress Cataloging-in-Publication Data

Names: Scott, Tim, 1965- author. | Clark, Joel N., 1976- author.
Title: America, a redemption story / Tim Scott with Joel N. Clark.
Description: Nashville, Tennessee: Nelson Books, an imprint of Thomas Nelson, [2022] | Summary: "Senator Scott is a rising star who sees and understands the importance of bipartisanship to move America forward. This book is a political memoir that includes his core messages as he prepares to make a presidential bid in 2022"--Provided by publisher.
Identifiers: LCCN 2022002122 (print) | LCCN 2022002123 (ebook) | ISBN 9781400236497 (hardcover) | ISBN 9781400236503 (ebook) | ISBN 9781400236510 (audiobook)
Subjects: LCSH: Scott, Tim, 1965- | Scott, Tim, 1965---Religion. | United States. Congress--Biography. | South Carolina. General Assembly. House of Representatives--Biography. | African American legislators--Biography. | United States--Politics and government--1989- | South Carolina--Politics and government--1951- | United States--Race relations.
Classification: LCC E901.1.S385 A3 2022 (print) | LCC E901.1.S385 (ebook) | DDC 328.73/092 [B]--dc23/eng/20220228
LC record available at https://lccn.loc.gov/2022002122
LC ebook record available at https://lccn.loc.gov/2022002123

Printed in the United States of America

22 23 24 25 26 LSC 10 9 8 7 6 5 4 3 2 1

This book is dedicated to my mother, Frances Scott, and my nephew Ben III. Mom, you have always been my greatest champion. Your sacrifice and unconditional love forged me into the man I am today. I continue to be inspired by how you serve and love. And Ben, you are a continuation of the story of redemption that has played out in our family for generations. Yours is a life well lived, a story of perseverance and grit, a snapshot of the best this country has to offer.

Lastly, this memoir is dedicated to the country I grew up in. Only in America can my story play out the way it has. This great nation is filled with stories of hope and redemption—stories like mine—and I am proud to be a citizen of these United States of America.

CONTENTS

CONTENTS

FOREWORD

1952

"Not like that, Frances. You need to grab it from the base and twist."

I watched as Daddy bent low and placed his fingers around the ball of cotton. In one smooth motion it was off the plant and in his bag. Daddy stood tall, placing his hands in the crook of his back, stretching. He glanced at me with a small smile. "You're just the right height for this job, Frances. You're cotton-sized."

One of my earliest memories is of my daddy's hands—the thick calluses an intricate road map of fresh scratches crisscrossing over the deep creases of scar tissue. He moved down the rows untroubled as the end of a boll carved a new red road across his knuckles. I cried when it happened to me, but Daddy was brave.

His scarred hands were strong. There was nothing my daddy couldn't build. He was what we used to call a "man's man." In this day and age, I understand that may not be politically correct, but then neither was Daddy. He lived his life by three rules. One, "Nothing is impossible." Two, "If you put your mind to it, you can do it," which when you think about it is another version of rule number one. And three, "If you fail, it's because you didn't work hard enough. You are the only person who can stop you"—another echo of rule number one. Daddy wasn't a man to suffer excuses. If you had an excuse for your inability to do something, well, then see rules one and two.

It was a tight circle of people who knew that my daddy never learned to read or write. His education ended in the third grade because my grandaddy needed help working the surrounding farms, and back then the world had no real use for an educated black man. Throughout his childhood, he worked those farms from before the sun came up until long after it went down—picking cotton, planting, tilling soil, feeding chickens, collecting eggs, and mending fences.

In all my days, I never once saw Daddy insecure or embarrassed. He knew exactly who he was, and he understood his worth. The callused hands were a physical manifestation of his value. And when reading or writing isn't viewed as a necessary skill, it's not something you were embarrassed about. Now, I don't mean to say he had no struggles. He was human, just like the rest of us. But he refused to be a victim. Honestly, he'd likely scoff and say, "Frances, I don't have the time to be anyone's victim."

I remember one time when I'd had a difficult day at school—I was probably twelve or so—and Daddy could see I was upset. After I'd made my case as to why I'd had the worst day ever, he said, "Frances, you can stew on the bad things if you want, but if you have any hope of moving forward, you'll need to learn to live with them."

Daddy knew all about "bad things." Born in 1921, he experienced a world far rougher than the one I knew. His was the world of "whites only" playgrounds, bathrooms, drinking fountains, restaurants, benches, and just about everything else you can think of. His was a world committed to keeping black folk down.

Daddy very seldom talked about his hardships. He simply didn't see what good would come from dwelling on them. But I recall him telling me how scared he had been to make the drive from Salley to Charleston, South Carolina. I was probably fifteen, and Daddy and I were making that very drive together.

"I was moving to the big city," he told me as we drove through the town of Ridgeville. "I'd spent most of my life working those farms, and I wanted to see the world. I wanted new experiences with new people. I wanted to find an opportunity just for me."

"Was it hard to leave the farm?" I asked.

"Leaving the farm was easy. It was the drive from Salley that had me terrified."

I'd made that drive a couple of times in my life, and I couldn't think what could be so bad about that two-hour stretch of road. "What was so scary about the drive, Daddy?"

He pulled over to the side of the road and put the truck in park. He turned to me, giving me all his attention. I knew this was not just a conversation. It was a lesson.

"We had to drive through the towns of Orangeburg, Bowman, and Ridgeville," he said. Even now, many years later, I recall an uncertain look in his eyes. "Back then every black person knew the police in small towns were going to pull you over for any reason they could."

Daddy waited a moment. I could tell he was fighting back some deep well of emotion.

"The stories were cautionary tales. While some people learned what roads had potholes or what dirt road to steer clear of in the rain, *we* learned what towns to avoid. Our brothers, sons, friends were beaten or jailed for no reason. Young men . . . lynched."

Daddy paused again. Looking back, I don't think it was fear he was struggling with. I think he was angry. Furious even. Furious that he'd had reason to be afraid of driving through a town. Then Daddy let out a long, deep breath and became himself again.

"Frances, the world is changing for the better. People—our people—are rising up all over this country, and justice is coming. I may not see full justice in my lifetime, and you may not see it in yours, but until then, our job is to hold on to hope."

Daddy leaned forward and placed his callused hand on my cheek. "There may be great evil in this world, but do you know what I see when I look at you?"

"No, Daddy, what do you see?"

"I see great light. Your mama always talks about the light shining in the darkness. I need you to know that we believe you and your sister and brothers are that light." He smiled as he looked at me. "Did you know you can light up an entire dark room with one small candle?"

No matter what my daddy faced, even when the world must have felt like it was crushing in, he had no room for hate. Negativity wasn't allowed under his roof. You can't be a light— you can't have hope—if you have hate. If you ask me, if there is anyone with good reason to be angry, it would be my father. If anyone had reason to feel like a victim, it was Daddy. If anyone had reason for despair, it was Artis Ware. But instead, he was hopeful. He still saw the potential for our people. He still viewed the world as the land of opportunity and great hope. I never once heard him complain about anything. And my siblings and I knew he wouldn't tolerate a word of it coming from us.

If Daddy was the backbone of our family, Mama was the glue. She had graduated from the eighth grade, and she helped Daddy with everything he did. She would read to Daddy and write anything he needed. She handled business as well as our home.

My mama was also a peacemaker. If you saw her today, she would welcome you like family. She loved Jesus with her whole heart and never missed a Sunday service until her final few years, when she was often too sick to go. I've always believed my mama sat next to God, because whenever she prayed, He listened.

And, oh, my goodness, could she cook. I can taste her collard greens to this very day. She was the essence of a Proverbs 31 woman. A Jesus-loving, peacemaking, business-savvy, child-rearing, chef extraordinaire!

In 2001, Mama died of Alzheimer's. As anyone who has lost a loved one to this disease can tell you, it's a hard journey. Very hard. And Mama's journey was no exception, but she had the blessing of Daddy. He built her a contraption for getting in and out of the tub long before those infomercial tubs were popular.

Holding her delicate hands in his, he would tell her stories to pass the time. My sister and I often tried to convince him to let us hire someone to help look after her, but every time we broached the subject, he'd angrily dismiss us. "I am here with her. She is my wife, and I don't need help looking after my wife." In the final months, he did finally allow us to bring in someone to help just a little.

Fiercely loyal until Mama's last breath, Daddy never left her side. I'm blessed to have been a witness to a love like that.

As the years passed, my boys grew, becoming young men. My oldest, Ben, went into the military and recently retired as an army command sergeant major. His is a beautiful life. A well-lived life. And he still has much to accomplish. Timmy went into public service and today represents the state of South Carolina as one of our senators. But then again, you know that already.

If you are reading this book, it's because you want to know more about my son Timmy. Trust me when I say I am one proud mama. Both my boys have gone further and dreamed bigger, beating the odds.

Looking back, I realize I've raised them with my daddy's three rules. As a single mother living in what you'd call low-income neighborhoods, I consistently reminded them of their worth. They repeatedly heard they could accomplish anything so long as they never stopped moving forward. It was *all* possible and there was never an excuse not to go after the impossible. The light Daddy saw in me, I now see in my boys. And I can't possibly express to you the emotions I feel when I think of how my boys are living out Mama and Daddy's hopes.

2015

"You'll never guess who I saw on the television today!" Daddy's eyes were bright with excitement.

I couldn't help but laugh. This was a conversation we had on a regular basis. Daddy was ninety-three, and he still could not believe it.

"Did you see Timmy again?" I asked with a grin.

"I saw Timmy again!"

Daddy would then recount every last thing his grandson had said on whatever news channel Timmy was on. Though Daddy couldn't read, he had a photographic memory, and there was nothing he loved more than bragging about his Timmy. Whenever he left his house, anyone Daddy met would quickly learn who his grandson was.

I have never seen a prouder man in all my days. Considering

where Daddy came from and what he experienced in his life, seeing his grandson go so far and accomplish so much was almost beyond comprehension for him. Until the day Daddy died in 2016, Timmy and Daddy were thick as thieves. They had private jokes and secrets. They would talk to each other through glances and raised eyebrows, and you never quite knew what conversation was happening right in front of you.

On more than one occasion, I tried to make Daddy slow down. Maybe it's just me, but I didn't think a ninety-two-year-old doing repairs on a ladder was a good idea, and I would tell him as much. He would comply, but always with an irritated look. Then, the moment I left his house, he would call Timmy on the phone. I already knew what was next. Within minutes I would receive the expected call from my son.

"Yes, Timmy. I already know."

"Mama, you really need to give Grandaddy some slack. He doesn't need to be mothered by his daughter," Timmy would say.

The fact that Daddy was calling my son to reprimand me still makes me laugh. But it's one of the stories my heart clings to.

———

When Timmy asked me to write the foreword to his book, I thought long and hard about what to share. The stories I could tell you about my son would fill a library, but I think what matters most is that he always had—and still has—the biggest heart of anyone I've ever known. He's always looking out for the voiceless, the folks who are hidden or left behind.

I wanted you to know my parents' story because I think knowing where someone came from helps you to understand who they are. I see my daddy in Timmy's eyes. He is the best part of my daddy and mama combined, but he is also so much more. As all children are meant to do, Timmy blazed his own trail and established himself as his own man. He is no longer just "Frances Scott's son" or "Artis and Louida Ware's grandson." He is Senator Tim Scott.

Every family wants the next generation to do better and go further than they did. My daddy spent his life pouring into my siblings and me so we could do more than he ever dreamed. I did the same with Timmy and Ben. When you look at the world my daddy was born into, and then jump ahead all those years to where my sons sit now, I don't think he could imagine a better story. And it's not over yet.

Before I leave you, can you do me one favor? I want to share a prayer for our country. I want to lift us up to our heavenly Father. My daddy believed in hope. I believe in hope. And my boy Timmy is working hard every day to make hope a reality for us all.

Dear, dear, heavenly Father, I pray that You would bless each reader of my son's book. Bless them with hope that comes from knowing that even hard times can be used by the Lord for good. I pray for our country to be the beacon we were called to be from our founding, and I ask You, Father, to help us to be the city on the hill that the world might look to for encouragement. I also pray that they would know my son Tim and his heart for all people. May his words bless them with his story of redemption so that they might experience theirs or find their paths.

Frances "Mama" Scott
January 2022

INTRODUCTION

When I sat down to write this book, I kept coming back again and again to why. Why write a memoir now? I turned fifty-six while typing these pages, and I fully believe I have many more years to grow, to learn, to serve, and to live out my story. Why am I compelled to spend the time to write about my life so far, when life is already busy beyond words? Why not wait a few more years?

I wake up every day with a dream for our country that I just can't shake. It is the same dream I had when I first stepped into public service in South Carolina back in 1995. In my dream, the American people are more unified than they have ever been. In my dream, a single mother has everything she needs to be successful. In my dream, our nation is woven together by our core convictions that transcend race, ideology, and any other societal markers of identity. My dream is that when we are under duress, we will turn *to* each other rather than *against* each other. Though I will explain how it came to be in a later chapter, the dream that motivates me more than any other is the idea that my life will positively influence the lives of one billion people before I die. I get that this might sound crazy, but the best stories always are!

Some will decry them as impossible dreams. Yet I know we can get there if we foster within ourselves a spirit of empathy, grit, and, most of all, hope. I know this because I have seen these realities play out in my life and in the lives of those around me again and again—moments of greatness when everyday people like you and me have created positive change. And these moments are not scarce. Every day, throughout our nation, miracles are taking place. These miracles manifest every time an American citizen sacrifices for a neighbor or for the ones they love. Each and every day there is a little bit of magic being woven into the fabric of our nation.

When I look at our nation, I don't see division. I don't for one second believe the false narrative of a racist, divided America that has been spun by big media. I see a tapestry of stories being woven together to form something beautiful. What I see are nearly 330 million souls who wake up every day with dreams of their own. And I believe the vast majority of us, no matter our politics or religious beliefs, are doing all we can to build healthy and strong families, businesses, communities, and, by extension, a stronger America.

In these pages you will not find a typical memoir. While I do dive into many of the most painful, pivotal, and profound moments of my own life, I've also woven a tapestry of stories from some of the most profound moments in American history. You'll encounter the inspiring stories of Jackie Robinson, John Wanamaker, Madam C. J. Walker, and Amos Humiston. You'll read about two heroic police officers who faced the impossible while trying to protect the innocent. You'll find my intensely personal story of the Mother Emanuel AME Church massacre in 2015. Through telling these and many other stories, along with my own, I have endeavored to tell the story of us, the story of

America. This is a story about finding our identity both as individuals and as a nation. And it is a story of redemption.

While I have great aspirations for this nation, I also understand that my time on this earth is limited. The unbelievable privilege of occupying the Senate seat I now sit in will someday belong to someone else. The honor of representing my friends and family, my neighbors, and complete strangers continues to be such a tremendous blessing. It's a blessing I sometimes still find impossible to believe has happened to this fatherless, poor kid who was—according to data, history, and experience—supposed to fail.

No matter where you may be in your journey, it is my sincere prayer that you will experience hope within these pages.

ONE

A GAME OF INCHES

1973

I couldn't tear my eyes away from the faded green shag carpet. Sitting at the end of the couch and squeezing my Dallas Cowboys football with every bit of strength my seven-year-old frame could muster, I knew it was my fault.

"You are nothing! Do you hear me?" My father was beyond angry. He was enraged. Spittle flew from his lips as he pounded his fist into the wall. "You leave now, and you will regret it for the rest of your life. You are nothing but a coward!"

I wasn't really hearing the words. I don't actually remember a single one. I only know what was said because my mother recently told me the whole story.

All I remember is the green shag carpet, the shouting, the sound of fists slamming into walls—and the conviction that everything bad that was happening was because of me. I distinctly remember the feeling of pressure, as if some great weight were pressing in on my chest and squeezing down on my shoulders, making it impossible for me to find a deep breath.

I hated the fighting even more than I hated the drinking. It was only midmorning, and though my dad hadn't yet cracked open a beer, it was just a matter of time. My mom was done. She simply couldn't take any more of the abuse. She opened the front door to reveal thick snowfall. She hesitated only a moment.

Mom had spent most of her life in South Carolina and had zero experience driving in snow. Cold wind blew into the apartment as Mom squared her shoulders and stepped outside. Dad continued his tirade of threats as Mom began to pack everything we owned into our lime-green Plymouth Cricket.

"I'm not going to let you take my kids away. I will take you to court and make sure you never get to see them again! Do you hear me?" he yelled.

I wonder how they made the carpet so fluffy like that. It was a stray thought.

"Timmy, get in the car. We need to leave now," my mom said. Her voice sounded distant as the carpet suddenly blurred. "Timmy, I need you to get up."

I crumbled. "Please, Mom!" I could barely form the words as tears streaked my face. "Please. I don't want to go! Please don't do this!"

I tried to say more, but I couldn't get the words out. My mom was not only done with the fighting and the drinking, but she had already cried all her tears, and she wasn't going to shed another one.

Mom glanced at my nine-year-old brother, Ben, who sat beside me. He also had tears in his eyes. "Help me with your brother." Ben stood and placed a hand on my shoulder. I remember weeping as I finally rose.

"Frances!" Dad's shout stopped all of us in our tracks. "Take them away from me and your kids will never succeed. They will be nothing, just like their mama."

Mom didn't turn around. She didn't look back. She merely walked out into the thick snow and climbed into the car. Ben helped me into the back seat before crawling in beside me.

Those words I do remember. *They will never succeed. They will be nothing.* I'd heard those threats many times before.

The image of my father watching us drive away is clear in my mind. He stood in the snow in his Army slacks and a white T-shirt. His eyes filled with rage.

As we drove through the thickening snowfall, I didn't blame my mom. She didn't have a choice. Though I didn't like the things he said and did, I still idolized my father, so I definitely didn't blame him. In that moment in my heart, a lie began to form that would define me for more years than I'd like to admit. *This is happening because of me. If only I could have done better or tried harder, my family would still be together. I. Am. Not. Enough.* This lie struck at the core of my identity.

I barely remember the drive to South Carolina after my mom left my dad. We arrived at my grandparents' place with little fanfare. As we pulled up to a small house on a dirt road, my grandparents stepped outside to meet us.

"Daddy," my mom said as she got out of the car. "I was hoping we could . . . I was hoping you might have room for—"

Grandaddy didn't let her finish. He stepped in and wrapped his arms around her. "Frances," he whispered in her ear. "You never have to ask to come home. What's mine is yours. Me and your mama can't wait to get to know our grandkids all the better."

As Ben and I climbed out of the car, Grandaddy stepped back from my mom and knelt in front of us. "It's good to see you boys again. Why don't you help me unload the car so we can get inside and get some food?"

I didn't know what to think about living with my grandaddy at first. He was quiet. I wasn't used to quiet men. Grandmama, on the other hand, loved to talk. She asked questions, prayed for us out loud every single day, and when she wasn't talking or praying, she was singing or humming gospel songs.

Grandmama cooked and baked and was so loving that it didn't take long for that cramped little house to feel like home. Though my mom, Ben, and I shared a bed, the lack of physical space didn't matter all that much. My memories of that time are almost all positive. It was the love of my grandparents and my mother that set the tenor for my day-to-day life.

After a few months, my father showed up at the front door. It was Grandaddy who answered, or rather, he was the one who opened the door. When he saw my father standing outside, Grandaddy didn't say a word. He simply stepped out and closed the door behind him. He stood there on the front porch, staring at my father.

"I . . ." My father cleared his throat, standing taller. "I need to see my wife."

Grandaddy just stared at him.

"Listen, old man. You need to go get Frances. I'm taking her and the boys home today."

Grandaddy took a step forward so he was nose-to-nose with my father. "I don't think I'm going to let you take them home today," he said in a voice tight with anger. "Or any other day for that matter. In fact, I don't think you are ever going to come by here again. Is that understood?"

My father was angry, but he was also wise enough to know

it wasn't going to end well if he tried to force his way past Grandaddy. My grandaddy was a formidable man.

THE DREAMS OF A SON

Even with the unbelievable love and support of my mother and grandparents, much of my childhood was defined by the words my father had shouted as we drove away. I struggled for years before I finally found the strength to truly forgive him. If I am honest, for much of my childhood, I was angry at my dad for all the things he did to Mom, Ben, and me. But even in that anger, I still craved his approval. Like so many children, I worshipped my father, whether he deserved it or not. In one of my earliest memories—I must have been four or five—my dad and I were driving across Kincheloe Air Force Base in upstate Michigan, where he was stationed at the time. Dad was chain-smoking yet another pack of Kool menthol cigarettes, although I had pretty bad asthma and even worse allergies. It was a brisk day, so he had his window open only a little, and the inside of the truck was thick with smoke. Even as I coughed and tried desperately to find my breath, I looked at my dad sitting there with a cigarette hanging from his lips and thought he was the coolest man on earth. And I was his kid.

Throughout my childhood, and even into my early adulthood years, all I wanted was to make my dad proud. Even after we moved and I barely heard from him, I had a vivid recurring dream of hearing his car drive up. In those dreams, he would arrive in his pressed slacks and, as he was silhouetted by the setting sun, would crack open a beer, take a long swig, and lean back against the truck.

"Son, I have to tell you, I drove in early and watched the

game. When you scored that touchdown, I have never been more proud to be your dad." Those words—even in a dream—were all I ever wanted to hear.

In a later chapter, I will explain how my father and I reconnected many years later and how I found it in my heart to forgive him and even forge a stable relationship. But it took a long road to get there.

When I look back now, I understand that my dad was not a bad man. He was a man who wrestled with his demons, and for a few decades his demons pinned him to the mat. He was a man who carried on his shoulders a deep and all-consuming pain I am only recently beginning to understand.

Dad wasn't just a Vietnam vet; he was a black Vietnam vet. The men who came home from that war were spat on. They were called baby killers. They left the misery and brutality of an impossible war front and arrived home to a nation that wanted nothing to do with them, that was embarrassed by them. On top of that, my father came home to a nation that wouldn't allow him to rise, purely because of the color of his skin.

To this day, my father won't speak a single world about his time in Vietnam or what it was like to come back home. It took him decades before he finally realized he needed help and that he'd been suffering from what we know today as post-traumatic stress disorder (PTSD). Back then they just called it shell shock, and it went almost entirely untreated. Besides the war, over the past few years I have learned a little of his childhood. To say it was hard, brutal even, is an understatement.

What my father went through didn't excuse him or absolve him of how he treated us. He was still responsible for his actions. But knowing all that had happened to him opened the door for grace to walk in.

DOING OUR BEST WITH WHAT
WE'VE BEEN GIVEN

Today, I have come to believe most, if not all, people are doing the best they can with what they have been given. We all struggle with our pasts, whether because of the choices we've made or the choices others have made that have affected our lives. Yet I believe to my core that even those who seem to be at their worst, those who for all practical purposes seem to be failing at life, even they are doing the best they can within their circumstances. It is this perspective that gives me the grace to look past their bad choices and see them as God sees them. Admittedly, I'm not an expert at doing this yet. Often I have to remember that God has given me the grace I need to walk my rocky path, so I should and can do the same for others.

We are all God's handiwork, and our lives are His canvas. He uses us to create works of art. Have you ever looked at a painting and thought, *What in the world is that?* To you, it looks like a mess. But to someone else, it's museum-worthy. Well, that's us.

Over the years, I have made decisions that have muddied God's canvas. I have failed and made mistakes aplenty. Yet I don't think God sees it that way. I think He looks at me with the eyes of a perfect Father and believes I am doing the best I can with what He has given me. And He sees you that way too. We are all museum-worthy in His eyes.

Waxing poetic about the American dream seems to be part of my job as a senator. But the concept is not nearly as simple as many of my colleagues like to portray. Every American starts his or her journey at vastly different places. The sky is not the limit for all of us. Some are born into seemingly impossible situations with no escape, while others are born into loving families with extreme means and influential connections. For black people in this country, the challenges are often greater, and their path is filled with more dead ends.

The American dream does not mean that anyone can do anything, that all options are open to everyone. Someone like my grandfather could not have bootstrapped his way to become president of the United States. Born in 1921, for most of his life, he couldn't imagine that his grandson would someday become a senator.

Here is what the American dream means to me. Every single one of us is looking up to have a better life. Whether you are a Wall Street trader or living in public housing, you can undoubtedly envision a brighter future for yourself. The American dream is not *fair*, in the simplistic playground sense of the word, and it is not a guarantee of success. Even if you do everything right, you may not achieve your dream. But that doesn't change the fact that opportunities to improve your life exist. The opportunities for a better life are real. The American dream is alive and vibrant wherever an individual has real choices available to take a step in the right direction and toward a brighter future.

Today, my father is proud of me. He has stopped drinking to excess and quit smoking, cold turkey, after sixty years of multiple packs a day. These decisions—and many others—have made me happy to be his son. I know now that even on the day we drove away in our lime-green Plymouth Cricket, he was doing the best he could.

The American dream is never realized overnight. It's not an event but a way of life. It is hard-fought on every front, moment by moment, day by day, year by year. Like football, my favorite game on earth, it is a game of inches. It's won by going forward and then sometimes getting knocked down when you least expect it. There will be setbacks along the way, but little by little we have the power to change our reality.

How do I know this, you ask? Because my grandaddy did it. Because my father is doing it. And because I am trying my all-out best to do it. Three generations of black American men have struggled, failed, and often made bad choices but, ultimately, over years and decades, have changed the trajectory of our family's path. I don't see my achievements as anything more than the continuation of my grandaddy's legacy. I am his struggle realized. I am the reason the pain he endured was worthwhile.

TWO

THE WRESTLER

1976

Watching wrestling alongside my grandaddy is one of my favorite memories. Grandaddy was totally invested and, therefore, so was I. I'd pull my eyes from the screen every now and then to look at his face. I didn't want to miss a single second of the fight, but I also needed to see my grandaddy's reactions, the wonder in his eyes.

What we witnessed was the sum of the best parts of every action movie and every redemption story rolled into a single event. The moves were fluid, perfectly choreographed. The determination of the fighters was stunning as they took hit after hit and refused to give in. What they endured should not have been possible.

When Bobo Brazil pinned Crusher Blackwell, I was on my feet with my arms raised. I looked back, expecting to see similar enthusiasm from Grandaddy, but he gave only the faintest shake of his head. That gesture told me everything I needed to know. *The fight is not over. Don't celebrate too soon.*

Slam! "One!" The referee's hand bounced off the mat.

Crusher was lifeless. Unconscious. There was no way he could recover in time.

Boom! "Two!" The ref's hand pounded against the mat. One more count and Bobo would take the win.

But with the ref's hand halfway down for the third count, Crusher revived, seemingly impossibly. He convulsed, throwing his body upward and sending Bobo flying.

Dumbfounded, I looked back at Grandaddy. His eyes never left the television. He merely grimaced and leaned ever so slightly forward.

Bobo leaped to his feet and stalked toward Crusher, who staggered as he struggled to stand. Suddenly, without warning, Crusher spun and swung his fist around with the speed and force of a wrecking ball. It smashed into Bobo's face, sending him into the ropes, momentarily stunned.

No! No! No! No! No! This can't be happening. I could feel my anxiety rising, but my grandaddy's composure never wavered.

Crusher Blackwell was not a man of honor. He stepped in, wrapped his hands around Bobo's neck, and began choking him. The ref tried to pull him off, but Crusher ignored him; he refused to stop. He was killing my grandaddy's favorite wrestler as we watched, powerless, from our living room.

In a panic, I glanced back at Grandaddy, but he showed no emotion at all. He sat perfectly still, tense as a bowstring.

I was still on my feet, adrenaline coursing through my veins. In a flash, Bobo was pinned. *This is the end*, I thought.

"One!" the ref shouted as I swallowed hard.

"Two!" I could feel the tears beginning to form.

Then the miracle happened. A split second before the three count, Bobo bucked free.

My eleven-year-old mind was blown. But before I could cele-brate, Crusher Blackwell was sprinting toward Bobo, throwing him into the corner.

"For the ride goes Crusher Blackwell!" the commentator's voice echoed across the room. Suddenly Crusher spun, shifting everything by using Bobo's momentum against him. The com-mentator's voice was filled with awe. "Bobo hauls him out of there. No! Reversal, and it's Bobo into the corner!"

Bobo landed hard with his back to the corner.

"And here comes Crusher Blackwell and—"

Blackwell staggered toward Bobo, who miraculously leaned into the corner and lifted his legs high, slamming them down onto Crusher's shoulders.

"Bobo, no! He goes for the head!" the commentator shouted in shocked disbelief.

Crusher staggered back, unsure of where he was.

The commentator's voice rang out, "Bobo on his feet. Bobo doing his thing!"

Bobo Brazil began to dance, mocking Crusher as he moved in for the kill.

"Crusher is on his feet!" the commentator shouted over the roar of the crowd. "Bobo, headbutt! Blackwell down like a ton of bricks!"

Bobo Brazil headbutted Crusher Blackwell so hard that Blackwell's knees didn't even bother to buckle. Felled like a tree, he slammed onto the mat.

"To the cover, one, two—and it's all done!"

I whooped and hollered and danced around the room in my best imitation of Bobo Brazil. My one regret about that day is I was too enthralled in the moment to look at Grandaddy. I like to imagine tears of joy in his eyes.

Grandaddy was fully comfortable in his own skin. He could sit silently beside you on the front porch for hours. Every twenty minutes or so he might retrieve his cigar and, when necessary, relight it. But even then, he never attempted to fill the void. His soundtrack was the click of the lighter and the slight intake of breath to ensure the cigar stayed lit.

While Grandaddy was a man of few words and held his emotions close, his love for wrestling was unmistakable. Inspired by these televised antics, my brother, Ben, and I often wrestled, mimicking the moves of Bobo Brazil, Rufus R. "Freight Train" Jones, "Nature Boy" Ric Flair, and our other heroes. As we flailed around the room, nearly breaking a leg on more than one occasion, we wondered how those men could endure so much.

For Grandaddy, they didn't come any better than Houston Harris. Born in Little Rock, Arkansas, the six-foot-six-inch, 270-pound phenomenon overcame all odds to reach the heights of professional wrestling. The world knew him as Bobo Brazil, the first African American allowed into the National Wrestling Alliance. Similar to Jackie Robinson, he provided a glimpse of what was to come—the world my grandaddy was striving for. His life would inspire generations of young African Americans. His success helped us to see that we could do more. We could be more.

THE STRENGTH OF A SEED

Next to wrestling, Grandaddy's greatest love was his garden. No matter where he lived, if he had a square foot of soil, he tended it with a master's hand. I vividly recall picking snap peas from the garden, filling buckets as we went. The garden was Grandaddy's happy place. I don't have a green thumb and can barely keep a weed alive, but working alongside him, I learned to appreciate the power of a seed.

Grandaddy taught me that the seed is infinitely more important than the soil. Sandy, silty, peaty, chalky—nothing deterred him. "Given enough time," he told me, "a seed will find its way through the hardest concrete." I didn't appreciate it at the time, but over the years that idea has become an integral part of the way I see the world.

Our country—our nation—is a living, growing organism. We are an impossibly intricate tapestry being woven every single day by more than 333 million Americans. I believe every one of us— man, woman, and child—is a seed. No matter the soil of our lives, our potential is far greater than our circumstances.

The men and women I most respect in this world are those who have overcome the impossible, like a resilient seed that finds a way to put down roots and stretch to the sun in even the harshest environments or a wrestler who overcomes impossible odds. Many of the men and women who make this country exceptional have been knocked down again and again. And when all seemed lost, they found the strength to carry on.

MORE THAN OUR FAILURES

Watching professional wrestling and tending his garden—these two activities are the things I most remember when I think about Grandaddy. Both activities reflected his priorities and beliefs. Resilience to keep going when the odds were stacked against him, and the perseverance to continue moving forward even when the soil was hostile.

Much of who I am today came from watching Grandaddy. In my life, I have experienced plenty of seemingly impossible challenges. Yet every time I've found myself in such a place, I remember my grandaddy. Even in the face of sure defeat, he was a man who never gave up.

Thanks to Grandaddy, I find it impossible to see myself as any sort of victim. Instead, I see myself as the seed that simply refuses to die. I see myself as the wrestler who refuses to allow the three count to land.

I may be stretching it a little to compare professional wrestling with a life well lived, but as a young man, I learned a great deal from watching it. My heroes on the screen refused to give up, even after taking a chair to the back of the head. There is nothing wrong with hanging on the ropes for a minute to catch our breath. There is nothing wrong with waiting for the two-and-a-half count before getting up. There is nothing wrong with tag-teaming out of the ring for a few moments to get our bearings. But as Americans, we stay in the fight. We don't give up. When we face the impossible, we rise above it.

The term "American exceptionalism" is ubiquitous in today's political discourse. It's a catchall—that is, it's equally useful no matter which side of the aisle you are on. I personally believe our nation *is* exceptional, but I don't turn a blind eye to our shortcomings.

This country has a provocative history. We have committed sins for which we need to repent, and we have much room for improvement. Like you and me, our nation is on a journey, and its story is still being written. We are an imperfect country in the midst of an imperfect journey, but as long as we are willing to embrace our worst failures and walk them through to triumph, we will continue to be exceptional.

Many in our great country want to point to the bad soil. Many want to bury themselves in our messy and sometimes unjust history. I don't believe the soil of any life determines the potential of the harvest that can be reaped. I choose to believe in the power of the seed. You are a seed. Every last American, no matter their failures, no matter their sins, has the potential to change history. Repent. Take an honest and accurate accounting of your life and then shine. Bobo Brazil did it. My grandaddy did it. And so can you.

THREE

TEET

1975

I ran out the front door of our second-story apartment in the Midland Park neighborhood. I was angry. I couldn't sit still. I was feeling something I couldn't clearly define. Today, I understand what I was feeling was a deep sense of shame. *How could it have come to this? We'd worked so hard, come so far!*

Shouts suddenly exploded from inside the apartment. I looked up in confusion. *What could possibly have happened?* The cheering continued as I scrubbed at my cheeks and allowed the faintest hope to creep in. As if moving in a dream, I made my way back inside.

Reggie, whom we called Hog, was on his feet, standing between me and the television. Darren was on his knees with his hands raised high, shouting triumphantly at the ceiling. Even my brother, Ben, had a look of wonder in his eyes, and he wasn't a Cowboys fan in the slightest.

"What, what happened?"

My question was drowned out by my cheering friends. When I'd run outside to flee from what I knew was coming, the Cowboys had been down 14–10 with only forty seconds left and the ball at the fifty-yard line. I was simply too anxious and upset to watch us lose. This was a divisional playoff game. If we lost, we were out for the year.

"Will somebody tell me—?"

Then I saw it. The replay. My favorite player in the world, Roger Staubach, darted back to the Cowboys' forty-yard line. Drew Pearson was in an all-out sprint toward the end zone. With only thirty-two seconds on the clock, Staubach threw his head back and launched the football higher and farther than anyone had ever seen. What Staubach and Pearson did that day has been dubbed the "Miracle Catch," and as I watched the replay again and again, it felt like a religious experience.

———

The two things I most remember about the early seventies are the Miracle Catch and what I call the "Miserable Miss." While the latter may not have the cultural relevance of the Miracle Catch, it was one of the more pivotal experiences of my life and defined who I was for years to come.

The Miserable Miss happened on a bright, sunny day outside my grandparents' house. Ben and I were out front, throwing a baseball. Ben threw a high ball that should have been an easy catch, but squinting upward, I lost it in the Charleston sun.

Thud!

Missing my glove, the ball spiraled full speed into my top two front teeth, removing them cleanly from my gums. I don't remember the pain. I just remember the copper taste of blood pooling into my mouth.

Luckily, these teeth were baby teeth, and once the pain faded, my mom wasn't all that worried. The problem came when my permanent teeth grew in. I don't think I've ever seen a more pronounced set of buckteeth to this day. To be honest, I don't actually know if the Miserable Miss had anything to do with my buckteeth. But throughout my childhood, it is what I attributed them to. They were so unbelievably pronounced that they had to be caused by something! My new, impressively prominent teeth earned me the moniker "Teet," which I would carry throughout most of high school.

What should have been a small thing, two buckteeth, became a defining aspect of my childhood. No matter what I wore, how big my muscles became, or how great my hair may have looked, all I saw when I looked in the mirror was my buckteeth. It took me years more than all my friends to find the courage to even ask a girl out. *Who would want to kiss Teet?*

1978

LIFE BURSTING WITH OPPORTUNITY

We were winning 21–10, and I'd already scored two touchdowns as well as made three crushing blocks. I was thirteen, and I had found my purpose in life. There was no greater feeling in the world than running up and down the football field while being celebrated by my coaches, my team, and my community.

I played for the Hillsdale Bulldogs, one of the best teams in the area. Coach Johnson himself had recruited me from my previous team, where we had earned a 9–0 winning record the year before. I played running back. Depending on the play, my job was to take the handoffs from my quarterback or to run down the field to catch the ball.

That night in Charleston was hot as the dickens. A steady stream of sweat dripped from my chin. While some of my teammates made a habit of complaining about the heat, I loved every bit of it. I never felt so much like a man as in those moments.

Thomas Griffin was my quarterback and good friend. In the huddle I could see the look of excitement in his eyes. The stench of sweat and grass couldn't hide the smell of victory.

Thomas glanced at Shawn, our halfback. "I want you to run faster than you ever have. I'm going to keep my eyes on you as if we're pulling a Hail Mary." Then Thomas turned to me and said, "Start out the same way. When they see you take off, they're going to expect you to go deep as well. Instead, let's try a stop-and-go on seven." Thomas clapped his hands, then everyone shouted "Bulldogs!" and made our way to the line.

As I crouched on the line, the cheers, the taunts, and the yelling disappeared. All I could hear was Thomas and my heartbeat.

"Set!" Thomas barked, and we dropped into our stances.

This has always been my favorite moment in the entire game. It epitomizes the best that life has to offer, bursting with opportunity. You know what you want to do, and it's right in front of you. Ready or not, win or lose, the waiting is over, and it's time for magic. Much of life is about being patient, waiting, letting things happen in their own time. But moments like this are what make life worth living.

I let out a slow breath to counter my racing heart. I glanced up at the face just inches across from me. I saw my own excitement, my own determination mirrored in Thomas's eyes.

"Green sixty! Green sixty!" His voice was loud and hoarse. "Seven! Hut! Hut!"

I exploded between the running back and the linebacker, sprinting just seven steps before stopping on a dime and spinning with my hands ready. I had barely finished the turn when I felt the football thud into my chest. My hands clamped around it and I turned to run. But before I could take a step, I was plowed into from behind with the force of what felt like a freight train. Up until then, I had never imagined a freight train hurting so much.

I thought the train had knocked all the wind out of me, until I hit the ground and three more bodies piled on. From beneath the jumble, one of the opposing players dug his cleat into my hand, pressing down hard. "Stay down!" he grunted as I screamed in pain. I still have the scar. And in that moment, I still had the ball.

Ten minutes later, I was on the sideline, shirtless with my ribs bandaged. The EMT told me I was out for the rest of the game. He said there was a good chance my ribs were broken, and it was simply too dangerous to go back in. According to him, the "time for magic" was over. As I watched from the sideline, the opposing team scored.

"Why are all your pads off, Scott?" I glanced up to see Coach Johnson standing over me with a grimace painted on his face.

"The doctor said my ribs might be broken, Coach. He said it wasn't safe to play."

"Is that right?"

"Yes, sir."

"What would you say if I told you the doctor who bandaged you up has a son who is playing tonight—on the other team?" Coach just stared at me, letting the words sink in.

It took a moment, but when they did, I was angry. I leaped to my feet and immediately started putting my pads back on.

"You can't let him play! He might really get hurt." I turned to see Coach's wife standing on the sideline with a look of concern in her eyes.

As I donned my helmet, Coach glanced at his wife. "Sweetheart, if your name was Tim Scott, I'd put *you* on the field."

We were magical after all. We went on to win that game by 21 points. In total, I scored four touchdowns. My ribs were just fine.

DISCOVERING OUR IDENTITY

My parents' divorce, my enormous buckteeth, and my ability on the field defined much of my youth. In a very negative way, the divorce and my teeth became entwined with my identity. In a mostly positive way, so did football.

As a young athlete, it wasn't out of the ordinary for me to score three or four touchdowns a game, and on a few occasions, I scored five or six. The better I became, the better I wanted to be. From my earliest memories, I slept with my football and carried it to every class. I needed to feel it in my hands. My football and I were one and the same.

Enough people cheered me on, and I was experiencing enough success that I began to believe maybe, just maybe, I could move from "really good" to "great," perhaps even to "exceptional." On the field, I was confident. Off the field, I was Teet, the kid who just didn't look right. You might think my football success would have overshadowed my deep-rooted insecurities. But instead, I played the role of two very different people. Neither role represented who I truly was. At that point in my life, the parts I played represented what others believed about me. With a helmet, I was a superstar. Without a helmet, I was a superdud.

It is easy to believe a lie. As a young boy, I believed my parents' divorce was my fault. As a young man, I believed I was ugly and would never have a girlfriend. As a young athlete, I believed football was my only ticket to a better life.

Belief is one of the most powerful forces on earth. Believe a lie long enough and it begins to define you, to change your identity. "You are not enough." "The divorce was your fault." "The abuse was your fault." "You are worth less as a human than others who don't look like you." "You were a mistake and should never have been born." "You are better than others at football because of the color of your skin."

On a grander scale, lies can and do alter how we perceive opportunities in this great nation. "Our country was founded on an irreparable sin, and therefore can never be good." "Our country has committed deplorable and hideous acts, and therefore we don't have the right to insert ourselves anywhere." "Our country is still fighting for justice, and therefore we are unjust."

Of course, we *are* an imperfect nation. But find me a nation or empire in the history of the world that got it all right. Aside from Jesus Christ, God in the flesh, no human has ever lived a sinless and perfect life. We are all on a journey toward discovering our true identities. One of the greatest sorrows I can imagine is those who pass from this life without ever having found it.

The power of belief is one of the reasons misinformation and "fake news" are so unbelievably harmful: they have the power to infect our self-image. With 280 characters your identity can be altered, transfigured, or even "canceled."

As a country, I believe we are fighting to discover and claim our identity. There's nothing wrong with that. As a fifty-six-year-old man, I am still learning who I am and what I'm capable of. I am still on the journey toward discovering the fullness of my identity. So long as I am willing to change—and believe me, sometimes I don't want to change—I will continue to grow. We, as humans, were created in the image of God, and while we often fall short, as long as we stay on this journey, we will be better for it.

As a nation, we need to stop the fearmongering and the us-versus-them conversations that aren't conversations at all. By their nature, they are battle lines. Yes, our country is still on a journey toward discovering the fullness of our identity. But that is the point. We are in the midst of a story still being told. Our identity is still being forged.

FOUR

Pivotal Moments

1982

I was singing Dazz Band's "Let it Whip" at the top of my lungs. The song had been released just three months earlier, and Charleston's WPAL radio station was probably playing it twenty times a day.

Grooving down the road in my mom's almost-new (we called it "newsed") 1982 Toyota Corolla hatchback and listening to great soul music is one of my happiest memories. As a sixteen-year-old, these moments of freedom were what I lived for.

When I came to the instrumental part of the song, I stopped singing and my eyes started to slide shut. I was beyond tired and should never have been behind the wheel. My eyes shot open at the sound of gravel under the tires, and I quickly turned the wheel and fishtailed back onto the interstate.

"Come on, Tim," I said as I slapped my face trying desperately to stay awake. I turned the air-conditioning on high and rolled down the window. "You've got this."

———

We'd just moved to Summerville, South Carolina, and we were thirty or forty minutes away from my mom's work. She'd purchased the car from Budget just weeks earlier. It had very low mileage, and Mom loved that car a lot!

Less than an hour earlier, my mom had awakened me with barely enough time to get out of the house so she wouldn't be late for work. I remember crawling out of bed, every muscle in my body burning from the constant two-a-day football practices. Like most mornings, Mom was stressing that I was making her late again.

I half ran, half stumbled to the door to the sound of her calling my name. I trotted out of the house still pulling my T-shirt over my head as I climbed into the passenger seat. Once inside I promptly reclined the seat back as far as I could and slept the whole way to Bon Secours St. Francis Hospital, where she worked.

"Timmy . . . we're here now," she said in a loving voice. "It's time to wake up for real."

I opened my eyes to really see Mom for the first time that morning. She placed a hand on my head and looked me in the eyes.

"You need to wake up." She quickly glanced at the rearview mirror to check her hair. "You've got an entire day ahead of you. Go big. Do your best. Make me proud." She was dressed in her nursing uniform and ready to go.

This was our daily ritual. Mom would worry over my tardiness and then over my tiredness.

"I love you, Timmy. Drive safe," she said as she exited the car.

"Love you, too, Mom," I responded as I walked around to the driver's side and headed back toward school for the day's first practice.

Besides the two-a-days and school, I also had a job at the movie theater in our local mall. I'd gotten the job at the age of fifteen, starting in concessions making popcorn and pouring fountain drinks. By the age of sixteen, I moved to the managing-tickets job at the seven-hundred-seat Northwoods Mall movie theater. Most days after practice, I worked from five to midnight and arrived home every night completely finished.

Was I exhausted? Absolutely. But I loved everything about my life. On the football field my star had continued to rise, and as a junior, I had caught the attention of some college scouts. The day I heard Presbyterian College was at a game just to watch me play was a very good day. It wasn't long before more scouts from other colleges were attending our games to get a better look at me. I could envision my future and it was bright. I would give football everything I possibly had. I would become one of the best. One day I would play for the Dallas Cowboys. And if they weren't smart enough to draft me, I would make them regret it every time they faced me on the field.

———

On August 27, 1982, I simply couldn't keep my eyes open. *Maybe another song*, I thought as I turned the dial. I grinned when I heard the Gap Band's "Early in the Morning." It had recently soared to the top of the charts, and I have always loved me some Gap Band.

As I drove down Interstate 26, I belted out the song at the top of my lungs because I knew Charlie and the band were counting on me, and I also thought it might help me to stay awake. I remember putting every last bit of energy into staying awake. But to no avail.

Rumble! Rumble! Rumble!

By the time I opened my eyes, I imagine five to ten seconds had passed. I was far onto the shoulder of the interstate when the loud rumbling of the tires on the gravel finally woke me. I was a young driver, and I panicked. Rather than slowly pulling back onto the interstate, I slammed on the brakes with all my might.

Though I am not certain, I believe Stevie Wonder's "That Girl" provided the soundtrack to what came next. As I slammed the brakes, I simultaneously jerked the wheel hard to the left in sheer terror. Rather than sliding to a stop like I'd seen in the movies, the car began to flip.

Stevie sang as the hatchback flipped five, six, seven times across two lanes of traffic. As I spun over the median, the windshield shattered and Stevie was silenced.

They say everything slows down and your life flashes before your eyes during a near-death experience. While my life didn't pass before my eyes, it did seem to slow down. My body twisted and my backside shattered the windshield. I grabbed the steering wheel to keep from being thrown entirely out of the vehicle.

"Jesus!" I yelled as I held on with every bit of strength I could muster.

When the hatchback finally stopped moving, it was on its side. I remember dizzily looking into the back to see the roof of the car pressing down onto the seats.

"I'm dead. I'm dead. I'm dead," I whispered as I noticed I was wearing only one shoe. There was so much blood. As I crawled toward the busted-out passenger-side window, I noticed several good Samaritans running my way. When I finally shoved myself out of the car and onto the concrete, I saw the car for the first time. It was easily half the size it had been just seconds earlier.

It was a miracle I survived with relatively minor injuries.

Mostly, I was covered in bruises and had numerous shards of glass in my backside. Even so, the accident caused me to miss seven games my senior year. Sitting on the sidelines and watching my teammates shine felt impossibly hard. I was happy for them, but with every missed game, any interest in a running back named Tim Scott faded, and my star began to dim.

I could feel it, taste it. Football was my way out, my way up. I'd spent years working for this. I saw the moment I bought my mother a house. I envisioned myself as the local hometown hero turned pro. Suddenly, all of it was slipping away through my hands.

1979

DON'T IGNORE THE HIDDEN THINGS

"Hand me that torque wrench," said Ed. His hand shot out from beneath the beat-up old 1973 Ford F-250. I knew very little about cars or trucks, but Ed was a master mechanic.

I walked over to his table and eyed several tools I didn't recognize. I knew what a wrench looked like, so I did the math and retrieved the tool that looked as if it could add some torque to a wrench. I placed it in Ed's hand and watched it disappear beneath the truck. A moment later I heard him using it. *Yes! I got it right.* I was batting fifty at best.

"Everyone has things going on deep down inside of them. Important things." Ed's voice was muffled from beneath the truck. "Big things. Just because they may be hidden to the world doesn't mean they aren't important." He slid out from under the Ford. "Life's a lot like that bolt I just tightened. If we ignore the hidden things, eventually they will cause real damage," Ed stood and grabbed my shoulder, meeting my eyes. "Make sure you don't ignore the hidden things."

"Yes, sir," I said.

I'd simply asked Ed if he'd ever forgotten to tighten something. I'd meant it as a joke, but in typical Ed fashion, he turned it into a life lesson. He could turn virtually anything into a life lesson.

Ed Bryant lived in the same apartment complex we did, and he was the head of the local branch of the NAACP. He was a role model to everyone in the community. Ed has spent his life not just trying but truly making a difference in the lives of everyone he has come in contact with. He fixed everyone's car, only charging them what they could afford—whether it was a dollar or nothing at all.

I first met Ed when I was eleven, and he has played a significant role throughout my life. I attribute a great deal of my political passion to the example he set. As a lifelong Democrat, he may have voted for me once or twice, just to show me he loves me, but we are ideologically very different. While we don't often see eye to eye on policy, Ed has always used his time, resources, and talent to raise up the next generation, and on that we can agree.

Ed believed strongly in his ideology, but it didn't define how he treated people. He could believe in something entirely different from you, but if you needed something fixed, a bolt tightened, a transmission replaced, his ideology took a back seat.

1981

MOMENTS THAT CHANGE YOUR LIFE

"You look like you could use a sandwich."

I glanced up to see a sandy-haired man in his early thirties.

He was carrying a Chick-fil-A sandwich. "Excuse me?" I said, confused.

"Come to think of it, I probably owe you a few sandwiches. Thanks for keeping my boys busy for me."

I immediately saw the resemblance. "You must be Philip and Brian's dad," I said as I extended a hand. In retrospect, I am quite certain John Moniz wanted to make sure his kids weren't hanging out with a bunch of scoundrels. He was a great dad, and that is something great dads do.

I was fifteen and working at the movie theater in the mall. I loved everything about it. Every day I watched men, women, and families enter the theater to experience another world. I have always loved the movies. While tearing tickets and making popcorn, movies like *An Officer and a Gentleman*, *The Empire Strikes Back*, *Caddyshack*, and my all-time favorite, *Rocky III*, entertained thousands. I understand the critics disagree. But at my age and my place in life, there was nothing better than *Rocky III*.

I remember the day John's kids darted into the theater. They were younger than I. Brian was ten and Philip was just two years old. The day I first met them, Brian was "chasing" Philip as the latter laughed and toddled into the theater. My coworker and friend Roger and I had seen them running around the mall a number of times but had never spoken to them. We were between shows and the popcorn was already popped, so we had time to talk.

Brian asked endless questions about working at the theater, and Philip was mesmerized by the sheer volume of popcorn our cooker could make at one time. They seemed to think Roger and I were the coolest people they'd ever met. I saw both kids every day for at least a week before their dad, John, introduced himself.

John operated the Chick-fil-A a few stores down from the

theater. He had a ready smile and was always kind. He also had what I considered the perfect life. His wife was kind, his kids were awesome, and his house was amazing. Whenever John stepped in, I would pepper him with questions, mostly about his life, and he was very intentional with his answers.

Over the years, I became an honorary member of the family. The more time I spent with them, the hungrier I became for John's knowledge. I was excited to learn how to become successful like him. And John taught me. But more importantly, he modeled a life well lived. He taught me how to give 100 percent each and every day. He taught me that success has less to do with talent than grit. And he taught me that sometimes giving the gift of a sandwich will earn you an eager audience for a lifetime.

MAKE MIRACLES HAPPEN

I just told you three stories that may not seem to have any connection at all: getting into a car accident, hearing life lessons from a mentor mechanic, and meeting a father figure for the first time. But when I look at my life, these three moments stand out as pivotal. They affected the trajectory of my life.

It is easy to fall into a shortsighted perspective of our lives and reflexively focus on our day-to-day routines: commuting to the office, pouring coffee, seeing friends, catching a movie, paying taxes. Each day indistinguishable from the next. But what is seared into our memories are the pivotal decisions and experiences: getting married, becoming a parent, getting a divorce, buying a car, a death in the family, an unexpected friendship, standing on a beach, climbing a mountain, surviving an accident. These are the most beautiful and most painful moments of life, and we vividly remember each one, whether we want to or not.

My life has been filled with these kinds of moments, and I have learned to be grateful for all of them, even the painful ones. I am who I am because of the beauty and the pain I have experienced. I am who I am because of the men and women who have poured into me when they didn't have to.

The memory of a nation works much the same way. You likely have no idea where you were on September 10, 2001, but I bet you know exactly where you were on September 11, 2001. You probably remember where you were when Hurricane Katrina hit. When the first African American became president of the United States. When George Floyd was murdered. When we left our citizens and colleagues behind in Afghanistan. When the Berlin Wall came tumbling down. If you are a little older than me, you undoubtedly remember when Neil Armstrong took one small step on the moon. We experience life in routine, but we remember life in moments.

We have all experienced—and will continue to experience—the unexpected and unwanted moments. For me, the two big moments were the day we left my father and the morning the brutal car accident took away the thing that most defined me, the thing I most loved.

But the moments I live for are the moments filled with opportunities. You and I have the ability to *make miracles happen.* We simply need to take that first step into someone's life. Ed Bryant and John Moniz stepped into mine and changed my world. Like them, we can mentor the next generation. We can volunteer at our neighborhood organizations and in our children's schools. We can serve, teach, mentor, and love those around us with abandon.

As a country we have the same opportunities, but on a grander scale. We have the ability to be the shining city on a hill, to use our influence to address injustice and our resources to invest in strategic partnerships that provide critical stability in uncertain times.

I believe with every fiber of my being that our lives are not defined by what happens to us but by how we respond. I have heard it said, "Average people talk about their problems; the great ones find solutions." How we react to the tragedies that befall us both individually and as a nation will define us.

This nation can still be the shining light to the world, but we must decide. We must act. And, most importantly, we must pray.

Clearly our Founding Fathers had some glaring blind spots, but they were smart enough to know it! They created a Constitution that allowed us to adapt and evolve. They had the foresight to allow for growth. The responsibility is now upon us to act on our opportunities. We can continue to build upon their genius and shine lights in the darkness, or we can allow the dark moments of our history and our present to define us. The choice is ours.

FIVE

TIM SCOTT FOR PRESIDENT

1982

The decision to run did not come easy. For months, I'd been asked again and again if it was on my mind. I'd sidestepped the question so many times I was beginning to feel dizzy.

Of course, I'd thought about it. Of course, it was on my mind. "President Tim Scott," I whispered as I lay in bed at night.

The idea of campaigning was exhilarating—the handshaking, glad-handing, and speechmaking. But I thought, *How could I possibly find the time? Besides, does a young black man running for president even have a chance in this environment?* Yet somewhere, deep down, I had a strong feeling I could do some good.

"I'm going to do it. I am going to run for president," I told my friend Donna Neighbors. "I've thought long and hard on it, and I want you to be my secretary."

"Timothy Scott," Donna said. "President of the Student Government Association for Stall High School." She pursed her lips in thought. "I honestly think you might have a chance."

"Stick with me, kid," I said with a grin as I placed an arm around her shoulder. "Together, you and I are gonna run this school."

Donna laughed. "I'd love to be your secretary," she said. "Although I really don't have any idea what that means."

"Me either," I said. "I think you're just here to make me look good or sound smart or something."

"Talk about an impossible job," Donna laughed.

The next few weeks were exciting. Back in 1982, Doc Brown hadn't yet coined his signature line, "Great Scott!" But when *Back to the Future* came out a few years later, my nickname changed from "Teet" to "Great Scott." It was a welcome change.

I believe it was Donna, though, who came up with our campaign slogan: "Great Scott for Student Government President." I don't mean to imply that Robert Zemeckis stole the line from my campaign. I am simply raising the question . . .

We made posters and pamphlets and recruited our friend Christopher Clark to be vice president. We also brought on a whole team of friends.

To this day, I thoroughly enjoy the energy of campaigning. It's a whirlwind, but it can also be extremely life-giving. Whether running for student government president or trying to hold on to my seat in the Senate, I feel an exhilaration that is hard to explain. Similar to lining up on the football field and waiting for my quarterback to call the play, running for any form of public office is a moment bursting with potential, bursting with opportunity. Win or lose, the waiting is over.

I've thought often about these kinds of moments and how many people spend their whole lives waiting for them. But magical, opportunity-laden moments seldom appear out of the blue. There are stories of powerful opportunities miraculously appearing and opening doors that had previously been closed, but those are the exceptions that prove the rule. Waiting around will almost never reap a reward.

WORK LIKE IT DEPENDS ON YOU

My friend Mark Batterson, lead pastor of National Community Church in Washington, DC, has a mantra that he lives by: "Pray like it depends on God and work like it depends on you." I love this! So many people miss out on much of the beauty and wonder of life, on much of the success they could achieve, because they are waiting.

Some of us wait because we're scared. *What if I fail? What if I try my best and nothing works?* These kinds of thoughts will keep us stagnant.

Some of us wait because we don't believe in ourselves. The opportunities to advance in our careers are there, but we can't find the courage to step forward aggressively and pursue them. And once again we don't move.

Some of us behave the opposite of how Mark Batterson lives. *Why hasn't God given me any chance to shine? I've been here praying hard for years now!*

The reality is, there are hundreds of reasons not to pursue something seemingly impossible. The very word *impossible* implies that pursuit is pointless. Yet I submit that what makes someone great is his or her inability to accept that something is impossible. A mentor once told me, "Write down your impossible goal. Then write down the fifteen or twenty steps, the things you absolutely must pursue, to make that goal a possibility."

He was right. Almost any impossible dream you can imagine can be broken down into several practical steps. Just look at what it took to put Neil Armstrong on the moon. The first impossible step came in 1903 when the Wright brothers invented the airplane. Numerous smaller steps followed over the next fifty-four years, leading to 1957, when a rocket launched Sputnik, the first satellite into outer space. The list of steps continued until 1969, when the world experienced the pure impossibility of the first moon landing.

Just look at any number of creations and innovations in the past century that have shifted the landscape of the world. Go back a hundred years, and ours would be an unimaginable world, beyond the wildest fantasies of those who lived back then.

In addition to learning how to make moments or opportunities happen, we need to learn to identify them when they present themselves. A failure is actually opportunity wearing camouflage. We simply need to train our eyes to see it. Had I not suffered a miserable loss when I threw my name in the ring for treasurer, I never would have stumbled onto the opportunity of running for the South Carolina State House. My biggest failures in life, played out over time, have opened more doors than I ever could have imagined.

Lastly, and this one is really important to me, I believe no matter how much success you have achieved in your life, it is your responsibility to make the moment, the magic, the opportunity happen in someone else's life. We are not on this planet to create tremendous wealth. We will leave it all behind when we pass anyway. We were created to be conduits of love, life, and liberty to everyone with whom we come into contact.

THOSE WHO THINK THEY CAN

I said before that I thrive on the energy surrounding a campaign, but I don't love the anger affiliated with campaigning today.

Running for student government president was mostly fun; there were far fewer daggers thrown at me back then.

In that race, my competition was a wonderful young woman who was very popular. Her name was Mary Ann Veloso, and we were friends. She was a smart, driven Filipino who was actively involved in pretty much everything around school.

I clearly remember the day when Mary Ann and I outlined our platforms to the student body. Mary Ann was responsible, serious, brilliant even. I stood behind the curtain onstage as she rolled out her plan to make the school a better environment for students and teachers alike. When she finished her speech, she retrieved her notes and exited stage left as the entire school applauded.

"And now we will hear from Tim Scott," Ms. Cabe, our teacher who was moderating the debate, said into the microphone.

I walked onto the stage to a smattering of applause. "Vote for Tim!" someone shouted.

I had scrawled a few lines on a crumpled piece of paper. In that moment, however, I had no idea where the paper had disappeared to. I stood before my school and lifted my hands wide.

"Who wants a free lunch for everyone!" I shouted into the mic.

The school erupted in applause, shouts of praise, and great guffaws of laughter. I glanced over at Ms. Cabe, who rolled her eyes as she tried to hide her smile.

I tapped on the mic a couple of times. "Settle down. Settle down," I said. "All right, in all seriousness, I really am a young man of substance and I have more to say." I leaned in with a very serious look in my eyes. "Lunchtime is far too short."

Again, there was an explosion of laughter. Even Mary Ann was laughing at this point.

By the end of the speech, I did say a couple of things that weren't totally jokes. I believe I said something about acting as a liaison to help provide better relations between students and teachers. But I think it was the first part of my speech that helped me get elected.

In truth, I quickly came to love the responsibility. While my platform had been more comedy than substance, once I stepped into the role of student government president, I realized it came with a great deal of expectation, not only from my fellow students but also from my teachers. To this day, expectation is one of my greatest motivators. The higher the expectation, the more motivated I am.

I am less of a people pleaser than what I like to call a "people prouder." I don't get upset when someone dislikes me or thinks I let them down. If I did my best and someone is disappointed, that's on them. But when expectations are high, and I meet or surpass them, oh, my! I love the feeling I get when the people I respect respond to the work I have done.

Apparently, I did well enough to garner the attention of my principal and the teachers. That summer I was selected to go to the American Legion Boys State. I had no real idea what this was or what it meant, but I quickly came to learn what a great honor and amazing opportunity it truly was.

Every public high school in the United States, except for Hawaii, sends two eleventh-grade boys to Boys State and girls to Girls State each year. These are incredibly selective programs that teach students how governing works. In that weeklong "governing camp," students are taught the operations of their local, county, and state government.

It may sound boring, but the experience couldn't be further from that. The way we learned these things was by running for and serving in elected offices. We held legislative sessions, court proceedings, and law-enforcement presentations. We created entire worlds and then governed them. The feeling at the camp was electric.

Just writing that paragraph made me realize how much of a nerd I sound like. To many, this may seem like a week in purgatory. But believe me, the entire week was amazing. The program was run so well and the teaching so engaging that even if you arrived with zero interest in politics, you would still be enraptured.

In essence, you learn through competition. And competition is my language. It's where I thrive. I didn't just learn what the mayor of a South Carolina city does; I ran for mayor and I won. In South Carolina, we have forty-six counties, so only forty-six boys out of one thousand were elected by their peers.

Getting a little cocky, I decided to run for governor. I had a brilliant idea. I was going to inspire every last boy in Boys State. I wasn't going to talk agenda or policy, I was going to shine a light, become a beacon of hope. And when I finished my speech, it would be a *Dead Poet's Society*–type moment. The other boys would forget their troubles, they would stand and cheer at the top of their lungs. They might even carry me out of the auditorium on their shoulders.

As I prepared to step up to the podium, I remember feeling unbelievably intimidated. I kept telling myself, *You've got this, Tim. Come on! You've got this!* My competitor had just delivered his speech. It was good. Really good. It dove into the real problems facing our state and gave practical and pragmatic answers. Even I had to admit it bordered on inspirational.

But he read a lot of that. He lacked eye contact, the audience connection. This thought flitted through my mind as I walked onstage. I knew I would not be reading from my notes. I had stayed up the night before memorizing the words. To this day, I still have them committed to memory.

I cleared my throat and tried to channel the greatest orators of our time, then began with a poem:

> If you think you are beaten, you are;
> If you think you dare not, you don't.
> If you'd like to win, but think you can't
> It's almost a cinch you won't.
>
> If you think you'll lose, you're lost,
> For out in the world we find
> Success begins with a fellow's will;
> It's all in the state of mind.
>
> If you think you're outclassed, you are.
> You've got to think high to rise.
> You've got to be sure of yourself before
> You can ever win a prize.
>
> Life's battles don't always go
> To the stronger or faster man;
> But sooner or later the man who wins
> Is the man who thinks he can.[1]

"That was a poem by Walter D. Wintle . . . and . . ." I looked at my peers staring back at me, and all I could see was confusion painted on many of their faces. "And I just wanted to inspire us all with his . . ." I cleared my throat. "With his inspiring words of inspiration."

Scattered bits of applause came as I exited the stage.

"Wow, man," said a friend who came up to me afterward. "That was sure inspiring . . . inspirational, really."

I tried to tell myself I'd done well, that I still had a chance. I did not. In reality, it was a terrible speech, and I lost the election. I got drummed. That one stayed with me for a while.

Looking back, it's easy to see why I picked that poem. I have always been an optimist and an idealist. Thanks in no small part to my grandparents and my mother, inspiration is one of my love languages. If I had been sitting in the crowd and heard that speech, I would have been on my feet in a flash. All these years later, however, I can admit that inspiration without practical substantive ideas is no way to bring about real change.

My experience at Boys State set me on the path to where I am today. I left that week having had the time of my life and with a burning desire to run for public office.

I remember walking back into my school after that week at Boys State. I roamed the halls and saw the staff with new eyes. So many teachers invested in me while I was at Stall High School. I was just one of hundreds of kids they saw every day, but I mattered to them. The opportunities the teachers—and my football coach—pushed me toward made high school a pivotal time in my life.

The idea that my school provided the opportunities for me to see what a career in public service might look like still blows my mind. My eyes were opened to a world and career I might never have considered otherwise. Yet isn't this exactly what school is meant to do? Over the last few decades, it almost seems as if our schools are trying to churn out responsible citizens as opposed to young men and women who are prepared for what's coming and are ready to take on the craziness (and often unfairness) of the world. Our schools should be preparing our young people to think for themselves as opposed to falling into groupthink.

It is precisely because of my experiences that I believe there is something purely magical about school. It is a time in life during which we are surrounded by friends, and the only thing asked of us is that we learn. We grow together as we integrate not just facts and information but also who we are and who we are becoming. Schools should be life-giving. Every last boy and girl in our great nation who attends schools, public or otherwise, should be ready to find and create opportunities that will launch them into a brighter future.

While I had many teachers I loved, it was Ms. Edgeworth who encouraged me to run for student council way back in the eighth grade.

"Tim Scott!" she called from the front of the classroom. "You have more of a gift for gab than anyone I have ever taught. Rather than using your gift while I am trying to teach, why don't you stay after class, and we can see if we can't find a way to harness that gift."

Instead of getting upset or putting me in detention, she encouraged me. I did stay after class, and that's when she told me she thought I should get involved with the student council. So I did.

Teachers have one of the greatest callings on earth. Throughout my childhood I had a number of teachers who didn't just impart information but championed me and cheered me on in almost every aspect of life. They were mentors who helped shape my thinking today.

Teachers play an invaluable role. Yet in many ways, despite the brilliant work of innumerable teachers throughout the country, schools are failing our children. Labor bosses have built their careers by making education far more about themselves and their power than the children they should be focused on serving.

Many schools in our poorest areas are simply failing. These institutions do not have the resources, bandwidth, or manpower to focus on innovation; instead, they struggle to perform the most basic functions. This isn't a secret. The teachers know it. The principals know it. The parents know it. But too few of them have the opportunity to do anything about it.

We live in a world where school boards are pushing back against parental involvement. And, in some cases, parents are actively being mocked.

In the United States, if you have means, you send your child to a private school. If you are middle class, you buy a house in a neighborhood with good schools. But if you don't have either resources or means, you are stuck. Your children are relegated to whatever exists in your neighborhood—and it's rarely good.

I don't mean to get up on the proverbial soapbox, but this subject is desperately close to my heart. I grew up in poverty in a single-parent household. I attended four different schools by the fourth grade, and I can tell you a thing or two about what I experienced in those schools. Yet I stand before you today as a member of the world's greatest deliberative body. Education was my ticket to a better life, and it can—and should—be the same for every child in America. In fact, I would go so far as to say that education is the greatest overlooked civil rights issue in our nation today.

My staff and my colleagues have heard me say it too many times, but education is the closest thing to magic we have in this country. At the heart of that magic, just like in so much of life, is opportunity. And at the heart of opportunity is choice.

We need to empower parents by giving them a choice. We

need to empower our kids by giving them a chance. Choice leads to competition and competition to performance. Choice is an integral component of improving our underperforming and failing schools. By introducing greater choice, we not only empower parents but also raise the collective bar on quality for public *and* private *and* charter schools.

Creating better schools allows for *every* family in *every* zip code to believe that the American dream is alive, well, and accessible for their children.

SIX

GRIT AND INNOVATION

1861

John Wanamaker stepped back so he could clearly see the sign above the door: Oak Hall. Choosing the right name had been much harder than he'd expected, but he was happy with the decision. *Oak* was the national tree of the United States. It signified strength and knowledge and was often associated with honor, nobility, and wisdom. *Hall* implied greatness, palaces, and grandeur. John had often read about the National Statuary Hall in the US Capitol, which paid tribute to great Americans.

Together, those two simple words, Oak Hall, promised much to the patrons who would soon pass beneath them. The inside of the store itself was a source of great pride for John. Every section was original; every department told a story. The men and women who entered his shop thinking they might haggle for a pair of slacks or a new blouse would instead experience something wholly out of the ordinary.

As for the location, John had searched long and hard before

choosing the corner of Sixth and Market Streets in Philadelphia. This address was directly adjacent to the site of George Washington's presidential home. It would be impossible for anyone to walk past such a powerful landmark and not feel as if they themselves were more than they thought. Whenever anyone enters Oak Hall, John imagined, they would know the history of our country was at their back.

The idea of Oak Hall had come to John nearly five years earlier, and it had taken him that long to get it ready to present to the world. He was staking his fortune on five simple words: "One price and goods returnable." How had he come up with those words? John Wanamaker was a devout Christian who believed that if everyone was equal before God, prices should be equal too.

Until John's innovation, shopping for anything involved haggling and bargaining. There was no such thing as a price tag. This revolutionary new price-tag system ensured fairness for all, no matter the size of your pocketbook. In Oak Hall, all the men and women who entered were treated as equals. Besides that, they were also offered returns—and John often had to explain this concept to some perplexed customers.

Other stores sold similar products, but John figured out how to do it differently, how to do it better. What he did at Oak Hall transformed virtually everything about the sales industry across the country and eventually across the entire world.

1887

ACHIEVING THE IMPOSSIBLE

Sarah stared into the chipped, rusted mirror for almost an hour. She'd never thought of herself as vain, but this was simply too much. She had all the proof she needed to know life wasn't fair, but this added insult to injury. She was going bald before she turned twenty-one.

Running a finger along her disappearing hairline, a tear struggled down her cheek as she pondered the misery of her life. Orphaned at eight, married by fourteen, a mother at eighteen, widowed at twenty. She scrubbed angrily at the tear. Yet she knew her life was no more tragic than anyone else's in her community.

At the same time, deep down, she knew something else was beginning. Something wholly spectacular. Sarah lived in a day and time like no other. Compared to the past hundred or so years, it was revolutionary. She could feel it in the air. The world was changing. Her parents had been born slaves. Her four siblings had been born slaves. She was the fifth and final daughter of Owen and Minerva Breedlove. And she had been born free.

The world was still unfair and desperately unjust. White folk walked around with their heads held high and seemed to think the job was complete. As if everyone could simply pat themselves on the back and move on from the stains of the past. This was, of course, ridiculous. Sarah couldn't help but acknowledge, however, that the world had been utterly transformed in the time between the birth of her older sister, Louvenia, and herself.

Ever so slowly a thought began to form inside her. *I will not be defeated by something as small as going bald. I will not sit here and simply react to the world. Not anymore. Let's see just how free I am.*

The next morning, she went to every beauty parlor she could find and took copious notes on many of the ingredients listed on their hair products. She asked question after question. Two of her brothers were barbers, and she grilled them on what they used and why. Something amazing was happening inside of Sarah.

She'd never had a dream of her own. Never had there even been the thought that there was an opportunity made just for her.

She researched and researched, then began to experiment. She wondered, *What happens if I add a little precipitated sulfur to some copper sulfate?* She studied her mixture, but it was too powdery. As she was thinking, a bee landed on her dress. *That's it! Beeswax will hold this together and form it into something malleable! What happens if I add petrolatum and a little coconut oil?*

Sarah became the guinea pig for her own concoctions. *Yes, this is good! But all I can smell is the sulfur!* Then a smile spread across her lips. *Violet extract should cover the smell nicely.*

A few years later, after experiencing no small amount of success, she married Charles Walker, who believed in and championed his wife with all his strength. Sarah decided to change her name and brand her hair-growth formula as well as her shampoo and soap under the name Madam C. J. Walker.

The women who worked for her became known as "Walker Agents," and they were loved throughout the black communities of the United States. In turn, they promoted Walker's philosophy of "cleanliness and loveliness" as a means of advancing the status of African Americans.

At the time of her death, Madam C. J. Walker was the first American woman of any color to become a self-made millionaire.[2]

1999

FAILURE BEGETS SUCCESS

Seven days and zero sales. For the second time in as many months, my heart was in my throat. Every insecurity, every doubt I'd ever had came crashing home. My brand-new agency had been open for seven days, and I hadn't sold a single policy.

Was it a mistake to believe I could do this?

Two months earlier, my career had hit a significant roadblock. An important step toward becoming an Allstate franchise owner was a proficiency test. Somehow I'd managed to fail what my boss had billed as an "unfailable" test.

It didn't help that, before taking the test, the same boss had told me I would never be a manager. "I just don't see it. You are a great team player, but it takes more than that to be a leader," he said. This had irked me to my core. But when I'd read the results of that test, I couldn't help doubting everything I'd believed about myself. Maybe I didn't have what it takes to be great after all.

The same night I learned I'd failed the test, my girlfriend showed me a drawing she had made of a large building with a sign outside that read "Tim Scott, Allstate." Having my hopes drawn on paper was like getting a tattoo. There was no going back. It was there for the world to see. The longer I stared at it, the more something powerful began to stir inside me. *This setback is not my whole story. Fine, it didn't go my way immediately. I cannot, I will not, give up.*

Allstate didn't allow potential franchise owners to take their proficiency test more than once. You were given one strike, and if you missed it, you were out. Yet when I asked to take the test again, miraculously they said yes. So over the next few weeks I continued to work and study. And I carried that picture around with me everywhere I went, just as I had carried my football everywhere as a student. I could envision it: the bell jingling when a customer walked in, the smell of the leather seats, the clasping of hands when I helped someone with a policy. I worked hard and I prayed hard.

When I took the test again, I didn't just pass, I was given my own franchise in record time.

The dream had become real. But my satisfaction didn't last long. When I opened the door, there was no jingling bell. And seven days later, we had made zero sales. My old friend doubt once again sidled up to me and sat in *my* leather chair. I told him he couldn't stay long, though. That first week of no sales tested my resolve, but thank goodness my resolve was strong enough to press on. On the eighth day, we made our first sale. It wasn't big, but it was all I needed to inspire me to keep pressing forward. By the end of the year, my agency won the Rookie Agency of the Year award for South Carolina. Goodbye, doubt. Hello, jingling bells.

That experience helped me to fully appreciate what it takes to make a business work. True, you have to pass the actual test. But the more important test is believing in yourself. When no one else believes in you, when the test results say you're a loser, when the drawing threatens to stay on a piece of paper, can you look past it? Can you stay the course? Or does doubt take up permanent residence in your life, leading you to walk away from your dream? Understanding the value of grit, the power of perseverance, is the true test.

BRIMMING WITH OPPORTUNITY

You might think the comparison between my story and the stories of John Wanamaker and Madam C. J. Walker is a bit of a stretch. But I couldn't disagree more. Tens of thousands of books could be written about so-called average Americans throughout history who refused to accept the world as it was as they pioneered their way through seemingly impossible circumstances. Our history is teeming with their stories. Most of them never make it to the surface, but don't be fooled—they are real. There are people with that kind of grit walking among us every day. All it takes to join them is a choice to become one of them.

Yet it is not simply our ability to face the impossible that sets us apart from other nations. It is the unbelievably innovative nature of everyday Americans. I can't think of an industry that has not at least partially been transformed by an American's inventiveness and creativity. Some of these innovations are as simple as hanging a price tag while others involve the creation of the cell phone or the internet.

Unlike any other nation in the history of the world, we are a country brimming with opportunity. Madam C. J. Walker was a first-generation freeborn black woman. That fact alone could have dictated a very different outcome for her. But in an unfair and unjust world, she discovered the magic that made—and makes—this country so great: *opportunity*. For all! No matter your color or creed, opportunity exists for you.

Could Madam C. J. Walker's life have been easier if there were laws in place to level the playing field? Absolutely. And there should have been. Had those laws been in place, I assume she would have accomplished even more with her life. But when is that ever not the case? Or you could look at it differently. Perhaps it was because those laws didn't exist that her grit was activated. Perhaps it's the barricades in life that make us say, "Oh, you think you'll stop me, eh? Well, watch this!"

Rather than focus on the very real injustice that saturated her life, Madam C. J. Walker focused all her energy, all her being, on every opportunity, no matter how small it may have seemed at first. In fact, small things can be great agitators. Think of that pebble in your shoe that slowed you down. Or that innocent conversation with a stranger who would one day become your spouse. That's the magic of small opportunities. It doesn't take much. You just have to find the courage to embrace them. Because when you do, it will always lead to more.

Every single one of us at some point in our lives will go through a dark night of the soul. In those moments, we can choose to wallow in self-pity or choose to dig down and find the grit and determination to be greater. Madam C. J. Walker chose to be a beacon for an entire generation. She chose to show what was truly possible when you refuse to give in, refuse to give up. Madam C. J. Walker is a hero of this country.

There will always be people who strive to keep you down. To give you a million reasons why you cannot or will not succeed. There is nothing impressive or special about naysayers. Shouting "unfair" at the top of your lungs is easy. Feeling like a victim is easy. Getting up every day and giving all you have to accomplish your dreams is borderline impossible. Even still, people do it every day.

I understand some people will read this chapter and think I've turned a blind eye to injustice. But I know there are men, women, and children who have been victimized, and it absolutely guts me to hear their stories. I have sat with those who have suffered at the hands of sex traffickers, and I have sat with the families of young men who have faced impossibly long prison sentences for relatively minor offenses primarily because of the color of their skin. I have sat with Walter Scott's mother and many others. I could give hundreds of examples of the injustices and evil I have seen—and experienced.

Yet, even in the worst darkness, I refuse to reduce people to the label of "victim." When I see those who have suffered injustices, I see more than a victim. I see an overcomer. Every person I've sat down with who has shared their story of injustice has always ended our meeting with another story. The story of being a conqueror. For this is how we are seen by our Creator—we are *all* conquerors. John Wanamaker and I share the belief that every one of us was created in the image of God. This means we have an infinite capacity to overcome, no matter the depth of the darkness.

This is not to say that I overlook injustices. I absolutely do not! If I could magically do away with life's injustices, I would. I simply choose to focus more on the conquerors, the overcomers who make our world a better place.

I have often expounded on the idea of the windshield and the rearview mirror. Just as our rearview mirror is a guide that we must occasionally check to drive well, our history is a guide that shows us how to live as better people now and in the future. But if we focus more on what is behind us than on what is in front of us, we will crash.

Injustice is real. But infinitely more real is opportunity. I believe there is more opportunity today in the United States than at any time in our history. There is more potential for Americans to rise above the fray and change not just our personal circumstances but our country for the better.

If John Wanamaker could do it, if Madam C. J. Walker could do it, and, for goodness' sake, if Tim Scott could do it, so can you.

SEVEN

THESE HEROES RISE

1984

I remember the mile-and-a-half walk from the theater. I spent the entire time thanking God for an opportunity that hadn't yet manifested. I prayed Matthew 7:7 over and over again: "Ask and it will be given to you; seek and you will find; knock and the door will be opened to you."

I uttered these words throughout the entire walk. This wasn't just something I wanted. I had dreamed of this moment for as long as I could remember. Today, I would step out in faith and change the course of my life.

I walked inside the office feeling nervous but also filled with anticipation and expectation. When I looked around, all I saw were a number of cute twelve- and thirteen-year-old kids sitting with their parents. I was the only black person in the office, and as a nineteen-year-old, I was definitely out of place.

After I took a deep breath, I walked up to the receptionist. *You know you can't afford this. Why are you even here?* I shoved the thought down. *No! Ask and you will receive!* I held on to this truth even though I knew there was no way I could afford it. I had the faith of a mustard seed, and I had to try.

You may think I'm being dramatic for characterizing the fixing of my buckteeth as "life-changing," but that was how it felt. My teeth were an ongoing source of misery. I struggled every day to look in the mirror. I may have been a confident, well-liked young man, but all I saw when I looked at my reflection were my enormous front teeth.

When I was growing up, I had many school friends who had braces. I watched in awe as, over a period of months, deeply crooked teeth were magically straightened. Never once did I dream of asking my mother for braces. I don't think it ever crossed my mind. We lived from week to week throughout my childhood. My mother worked harder and more hours than any parent I knew just to put food on the table and a roof over our heads.

When I was nineteen, I was working seventy hours a week at the theater. While I had saved a little, a large portion of every paycheck went toward helping with rent and groceries.

As I approached the front desk, I felt as if I were walking into a church. This was a holy place, a place with the power to change lives. The name on the placard next to the receptionist read "Dr. Monte S. Harrington: Orthodontist."

"Good afternoon," the receptionist said. "Do you have an appointment?"

I took a deep breath as I stepped forward. "No, ma'am," I said. "I just wanted to talk to an orthodontist. I wanted to see what it would take to fix my teeth." Even though I'd had these teeth since I was eight, I struggled to keep my lips closed as I spoke, feeling a deep sense of embarrassment as I stood before the receptionist.

"Of course!" she said cheerily. "That's exactly what we do here. My name is Becky, by the way. You don't need to call me ma'am."

"Hi, Ms. Becky," I said as I extended a hand. "I'm Tim."

She laughed as she took my hand. "I am not *that* much older than you! Becky will do just fine."

"All right," I laughed. "Becky it is."

A few minutes later, I was lying back while Dr. Harrington inspected my teeth. Though he didn't say a word, the wide-eyed look in his eyes said it all. My teeth were exactly as crooked and pronounced as I knew they were.

"How old are you, son?"

"Nineteen, sir."

"I'm guessing you don't have insurance?"

"No, sir."

Dr. Harrington sat back, pushing a button so the seat brought me upright.

"Listen to me, Tim. Whatever it takes, we're gonna make you feel good about what you see in the mirror," he said with a sense of urgency.

I just sat there looking at him, unsure as to what he was actually saying.

"How much can you afford monthly? Think about it and make sure you can actually afford it. And whatever that amount is, you have my word that it is all I'll take from you until the day we take the braces off."

"I . . . I'm not sure, sir," I said as the world seemed to spin. "Um, maybe forty?"

"Perfect! Forty it is." Dr. Harrington turned and grabbed something from a tray. "Should we get started?"

When I think back on this memory, not for one second did

Dr. Harrington or Becky make me feel like a poor kid with no insurance. More than anything, I felt respected. At no point over the year or so I wore the braces was I treated differently. I was never made to feel like Dr. Harrington was doing me a favor or having mercy on me. He was absolutely professional and clearly loved his job.

I don't know that I can adequately communicate the importance of this. It wasn't an old white guy taking pity on a young black kid. It was an orthodontist who saw an opportunity to fix someone's smile and improve their confidence.

My monthly payment to Dr. Harrington was one of the most important payments I made each month. And though it truly was a lot of money back then, I was proud every time I made the payment.

I remember walking home that first day with an enormous smile. I'd never been so proud to show my teeth to the world. The miracle had begun. I simply couldn't believe it. I was more excited about these braces than anything else in the short history of my life.

Throughout the next year or so, Becky and I became close friends, and I learned more about Dr. Harrington. He suffered from ankylosing spondylitis, which is a spinal disorder that causes the vertebra in the neck to fuse over time. I know it was painful for him, yet he never once let the pain stop him or get in the way of his cheery disposition. I have often wondered if this pain helped him recognize the need for an extra helping of grace in the world.

I clearly was a young man in need of grace, and he extended it happily. Although Dr. Monte Harrington died in 2014, I still think of him often. Redemption comes in many forms, and Dr. Harrington gave me a gift more valuable than almost anything else: he restored my confidence. In truth, I try to be like him.

He was an amazing man, and I think a lot of Americans are like Dr. Harrington. We are a people who extend grace to each other. All across our nation, men, women, and children daily live lives painted by the brush of grace.

If you want to understand why I believe we are better together and why my focus is on building bridges, you just need to look at the fact that bridges were built for me. Throughout my life, numerous men and women have stepped in to help me overcome some of the greatest obstacles a person could face, and in so doing they have become a part of my story of redemption.

1998

WHAT INTEGRITY LOOKS LIKE

Al couldn't stop laughing. He wasn't being mean; he doesn't have a mean bone in his body. But he was laughing hard—at me.

"I have never seen a man work so hard at something so impossible," he said as he wiped a tear from his eye. He knelt beside me to gather the eight or nine ruined nails at my feet.

"You told me to fasten the two-by-four to the wall," I said defensively. "And then you gave me a hammer!"

Al burst into laughter again. "I gave you the hammer because every grown man should own one. I did not give you a hammer to try to pound nails into concrete." Al chuckled as he walked over to the pile of tools and retrieved a drill. "This here is a hammer drill," he said. "Not to be confused with a hammer." He then began to drill the two-by-four into the concrete.

Al is the very definition of a jack-of-all-trades, except in his case he is also a master of many. He knows enough about building, plumbing, electrical, and landscaping that he is the first guy

I call when I need to fix pretty much anything. He is also the first guy I call when I need advice on business, my taxes, and pretty much anything else I can think of.

Al was the reason I was able to launch my own Allstate branch. I'd been working as an Allstate agent for a few years, and though I was making a decent living, I believed I was ready for more responsibility. When I'd entered the bank, I was wearing the best suit I owned. I walked tall and made sure my handshake was firm. I looked the bank manager in the eye, and I spoke with confidence, painting a picture of my success so far and projecting an image of my future grandeur.

The bank manager listened, nodding at all the appropriate places. But when I asked for a $40,000 loan, I was almost laughed out of the building. I don't blame the bank. I had pretty much no credit history, and my only collateral was a Nissan 240SX with 250,000 thousand miles on it. I left feeling more than a little deflated.

When Al heard that my dreams had run into a roadblock, he didn't hesitate. "Tim, I believe in you. How about I just invest $40,000 into your business, and I'll take a percentage of the company?"

I honestly didn't know how to respond. Nobody gives a kid with no background and no real management experience $40,000 to start a business.

In all my life, I have never met anyone as wise or gracious as Al Jenkins. Not only did he lend me the money, but he spent an entire week helping me build four office areas in the twelve-hundred-square-foot space that his money helped me obtain. Rather, I should say that I helped Al. I am about as handy with tools as a twelve-year-old.

The first time I met Al, I had been selling life and health insurance. This was my first job out of college, my first job as a grown man, and I was desperate to succeed. Al was one of my first big sales. He was also the most important sale of my life.

Al was working in his office when I stood at the door in my suit with my heart pounding loudly in my chest. "Good morning, sir," I said, trying to sound as confident as ever. "I was wondering if I could have a few minutes of your time. I am selling life and health insurance, and I—"

"Great. I'm in. Where do I sign?" Al interrupted.

"What?"

"My wife and I were just talking about the need for insurance. Listen, we just adopted a couple of little girls and one of them has asthma. Do you think we can get her covered as well?"

"Ah, well, yes, sir. If you give me a little more information, I think I can get right on that."

"Great. Call me Al."

A week or so after I'd set Al and his family up, I received a call. "Tim! Me and the missus want to have you over for dinner. What do you say?"

"I'd love to. That sounds amazing. When are you thinking?"

"Robin just put a plate down for you. You need to get here soon or its gonna get cold."

"You want me to come right now?"

"You holdin' out for a better offer?"

"Ah, no. I'm on my way!"

Dinner with Al and Robin was amazing. Their kids were so much fun. Eleven-year-old David wanted to tell me all about his favorite toy and five-year-old Sherry made lots of jokes. Katie was one year old and was doted on by everyone. Sitting at the table, I felt as if I were watching a three-ring circus. Al and Robin made me feel like part of the family.

This first dinner turned into a second and then a third. Before long, I was a regular in the Jenkins household. Every Wednesday night, after cleaning up the dishes and helping put the kids to bed, Al and I would sit in his living room and talk for hours. I would take notes about our conversations in a yellow notepad.

On these evenings, Al and I would address the ills of society, the inconsistency of the application of the rule of law, the challenges faced by minorities, the low expectations and suspicion surrounding individuals in minority communities. We would talk about the great progress we saw in numerous areas of our society, about the greatness of America and our role in adding to the collective story of our nation, about personal responsibility, about running successful businesses, and about our faith.

To be honest, I don't know why we were trying to solve the problems of the world. But there was something magical about spending our evenings together and planning to make the world a better place, even if we hadn't yet discovered how we would go about it.

———

Today, I marvel as I look back on those magical evenings. Though I had no idea at the time, they were the seeds of what was to come. I still go back to my stack of more than sixty yellow pads and look through the notes from time to time. Many of the things I wrote down twenty or so years ago are still inspiring the way I approach my job today.

Although Al is only ten years my elder, he has absolutely played the role of mentor, even a father figure, in my life. The more I watched him, the more I wanted to be like him. I wanted to have a business like he had. I wanted to have the success that he had. More than anything, I wanted to be the man of integrity that he was. Al isn't the kind of guy to preach at you. Instead, you experience what integrity truly looks like as he models it for you. It's catching. All you want to do is try to imitate him.

When we first met, I'd had no real business experience. Every time I made a sale and came home with just a little extra cash, I found a way to spend it. If I had a few extra dollars, I would show up at Al and Robin's in a nicer suit. If I made a few hundred extra dollars, I would upgrade to a new apartment I couldn't afford. If I made a few thousand extra dollars, I would upgrade to a car I didn't need.

I wanted the world to know about every last bit of success I experienced. And for me that meant spending every last dollar I made. The idea of a savings account was something I always put off. I told myself I would start saving in a few years, after I'd made a lot more money.

But Al was the opposite. His business was growing so rapidly it was hard for him to keep up. Yet no matter how many people he hired, no matter how much success he created, his lifestyle never changed. It took me a few years of watching him to get it, but this was one of the best lessons I ever learned as a young businessman.

I agree with the old saying that leadership is not taught, it's caught. Hang around with great leaders, with men and women of integrity and high moral character, and you can't help but start to be like them.

Because of who Al was and continues to be in my life, I am always on the lookout for someone in need of a mentor. Thankfully, over the years, it hasn't been hard to find young people who are hungry to learn. One of my great joys in life is channeling Al Jenkins as I endeavor to mentor the next generation.

I honestly believe I would not be a senator without Al Jenkins. Without the $40,000 he invested in me, I never would have had the bandwidth to dream about or run for anything. With his help, I created a successful business that helped launch me in a new direction.

I write a lot about opportunity in this book. I believe the miracle of opportunity is one of the things that sets the United States apart from the rest of the world. Brilliant, entrepreneurial, creative, driven self-starters are born every day all around the world. Yet, in most countries, these things don't lead to a better life.

You could be the most driven and innovative person on earth, but without an opportunity to invest your talent, time, and treasure, your giftings will lie dormant. We have been heralded as "the land of opportunity," and this is a very apt description. For me, even with a good education and living in a nation brimming with opportunities, I still needed the help of my community.

No matter how incredible our country is, it is the people in it who make the difference. It is the Al and Robin Jenkinses of this world who are pouring into and raising up the next generation while quietly living their lives.

1999

WHEN DREAMS DIE

I've had a dream ever since I was a young boy. I planned to use football to become rich and famous. Sure, a lot of that dream was about me. But deep down, more than anything, I wanted to make enough money so I could buy a house for my mom.

This is not a new thing. I may be wrong, but this seems to be more of a poor black boy's dream than anything else. I have met more African American kids over the years than I could count, and they all have the same dream. My theory is that it's because many of us were raised by single mothers, and we grew up watching them sacrifice every single day so we could succeed. The idea of buying a house for our moms is the grandest way we can imagine to let them know we recognize and appreciate their sacrifice.

My family mostly lived in small apartments in marginalized neighborhoods. The idea of painting a wall never crossed our minds. Even hanging pictures had to be thought through. Putting holes in the walls might come back to bite you when you moved out.

When I was growing up, my mom worked most nights late into the evening. And it wasn't always safe to park and walk to our apartment at night. That's why my dream wasn't just to buy a house for my mom but to buy a house with a garage for her. I can't tell you how many nights I lay awake imagining driving her into a garage and then handing her the keys to the house. I imagined the tears, the joy.

Looking back now, I understand these dreams are as much about the dreamers as they are about their mothers. The idea that Mom knows I was successful enough to do something like this—what child doesn't want to feel that kind of pride from their parent?

My dream died when my chance at a football career died. But the dream was resurrected again when my Allstate branch didn't just do well but outperformed my greatest expectations.

We were breaking sales records every month. The agency did so well that two of my managers ended up leaving to launch their own branches.

The day my dream came true is forever seared into my memory. I drove my mother into the garage of her new home, turned to her, and handed her a set of keys. As we climbed out of the car, the look on her face was one of pure wonder.

As we entered the house through the laundry room and walked around the nearly eighteen-hundred-square-foot house, my mother wept. So did I. We talked about the colors she might paint the walls. We dreamed about where we could place book-shelves and hang pictures. It was one of the most important days of both of our lives.

It's been fourteen years now, and Mom still loves that house. She is highly involved in her church and often uses the spacious living room as her prayer room.

This moment was the fruit of a dream I'd carried for as long as I can remember. But this moment was possible only because of the nation in which I was born.

There are single mothers all across this great country. They are working impossible hours while trying to raise their children. This is often a thankless challenge. Still, every single day these heroes rise. If you are a single mother and you are struggling, if you are wondering if your sacrifice is worth it, I am living proof that it is. Keep going. Hang on. Your sacrifice means everything, and though your kids might not see it now, they will.

We have a system where you are rewarded for your efforts. As Americans, with enough hard work, we have the opportunity to see our wildest dreams become realities. Hollywood isn't the only place happy endings exist. The story line can be just as real for poor kids in single-parent households who are desperate for a way out.

In many ways, I believe in redemption, not simply because I'm an eternal optimist, but because I've experienced it. And I've experienced it because I live in this great nation.

As I've said before, our systems are not perfect, but our Founding Fathers had incredible foresight. They knew free markets were essential to economic progress. Unlike so many places around the world, in the United States *anyone* can climb the economic ladder. There are those who argue that certain members of society have an advantage—a head start on the climb—and I don't discount that. But, at the same time, *every person* has the opportunity to climb all the way to the top of their own American dream.

We have to be willing to take that first step. Redemption doesn't just happen. We are meant to play a role in our redemption stories. We need to step out, step up, and do everything in our power to change the trajectory of our lives.

1994

WHEN LOSS BECOMES A BLESSING

One of my big motivations for running for public office came when I heard the news that the 1993 Base Realignment and Closure Commission (BRAC) had decided to shut down the Charleston Naval Shipyard. This news was a major blow to the South Carolina economy.

The Charleston Naval Shipyard was the largest employer of civilians in the state. Built in 1901, it had an enormous impact on the local community, the tri-county area, and the entire state. Over the years, hundreds of thousands of people were employed, 256 vessels were built, and countless millions of dollars were poured into the state's economy by the shipyard. And with the devastating announcement came the forecast of double-digit unemployment.

I remember reading the news and feeling unbelievably motivated to help fix all the problems this closure would cause. Furthermore, when I looked at my community, there were several things happening that needed to be addressed, that needed to change. The only way I could think to change them was to have a seat at the table with those who were making the decisions.

Over time, as it is with most perceived losses or failures, losing the naval facility became a blessing. As a city, Charleston was forced to reinvent itself, to become more independent. When I ran for Charleston County Council in 1994, I ran on the premise of diversifying our economy to include a Class A industrial park. We would no longer be dependent on the government dole. We would attract and recruit diverse businesses to our great city. And, over the years, that is exactly what we did.

Believe it or not, I first walked into the Democratic Party offices. I had decided from the start I was going to visit both the Democrat and Republican offices. I entered the Democrat office not because our ideals or values lined up but because the assumption was that if you were black in South Carolina, you were a Democrat. Back then, I felt my political affiliation had less to do with my ideology than it did with my identity.

When I walked into the Democratic Party offices, I was told I needed to wait my turn and go to the back of the line.

The very next day, I attended the monthly meeting held by the Republican Party and told the group what I hoped to accomplish. One of the members of the county council party looked at me and said, "Tim, there's never been a black Republican elected. But I like what you're about, so if you want to try, I say go for it."

Over the next month, the news got out that a young black man was running as a Republican. The reception of the news was mostly positive. Henry McMaster, the chairman of the Republican Party in South Carolina at the time, reached out and asked if I would be willing to meet.

I remember the day Joe McKeown, one of my closest friends since my midtwenties, and I made the drive to the Republican Party headquarters in Columbia. It was raining hard. On the way I was feeling excited about the steps I was taking, but I was also a little hesitant.

"Tim," Joe said, "you are more than prepared for this. More than anyone I have ever known, you were created to enact change."

Joe had been my personal trainer for a few years before coming to work with me at Allstate. We actually became partners, and eventually he left to operate his own branch. Since the day I first dipped a toe into politics, Joe has been at my side. He is my senior advisor, and when it comes to my role as an elected official, he is the person I turn to when I need to strategize or talk through something.

Joe continued, "I don't care what anyone says. Simply because it has not been done before doesn't mean that it cannot be done! You are going to shatter this glass ceiling, and you won't stop there."

Joe also plays the very important role of encourager in my life. Everyone needs a friend like Joe McKeown.

I remember sitting in a room with Henry McMaster and his team. Henry wanted to hear my story. As I told him who I was and what I believed in, his eyes lit up.

"I gotta be honest," he said when I was finished. "I don't just think you are going to win. I think you are going to win big."

Henry was right. I ran against Floyd Craven for the position of county councilman and won the seat handily, beating him with 72 percent of the vote.

Since then, I have run for a number of offices successfully, but I have also suffered a colossal loss. One year after stepping into the role of county councilman, I made the decision to run for the state senate. I was told by my closest friends that there was zero chance I could win. Yet I prayed about it and believed this was my moment. Although any first grader could see the writing on the wall, I decided to throw a Hail Mary. I wish I could tell you this was my Roger Staubach moment. But, in the end, I was defeated 65 percent to 35. It was a shellacking, and it took me a while to get over it.

I've written a couple of books about the crazy journey that brought me to the US Senate. It is an impossible story. Similar to managing a successful business or buying my mom a house, my story is about as American as it gets. And it is possible only because I grew up in this great nation.

I am a US senator for this one reason. It is the thing that drives me every single day. I am doing my all-out best to make the kinds of opportunities that were presented to me more readily available to every American, no matter their zip code. While I believe we live in a nation that's already brimming with opportunity, I also believe one of the primary jobs of the federal government is to make sure these kinds of opportunities exist for everyone.

EIGHT

CHAMPION OUR DIFFERENCES!

1998

"Knock, knock," I said, as I entered my grandparents' house. "I brought some groceries." I walked straight through to the kitchen and placed the bags on the counter.

"You'll never guess who I ran into at the store," I said as I began unpacking. "Do you remember . . ." As I turned, I immediately lost my thought. Grandaddy stood at the entry to the kitchen, gripping the wall so tight I was surprised it wasn't crumbling.

"Timmy, you need to go talk to your grandmama." Fear painted his face as he walked stiffly over to the kitchen table, sitting down hard. "I can't seem to . . . I can't . . ."

I didn't hesitate. "Grandmama?" I called as I anxiously darted into the small living room. I stopped for a moment. Grandmama was sitting in her favorite chair. Her back was to me, and she was facing the window. Taking a deep breath, I continued forward and knelt beside her. "How are you doing, Grandmama?" I said as I placed my hand over hers.

After a moment she turned and met my eyes. I searched for even the smallest sign of recognition, for any awareness that she knew me, but there was none.

"Grandmama, it's me, Timmy." I blinked back tears as I continued searching her face.

She stared blankly, not seeming to see anything at all.

Please, God, not yet! I thought. I retrieved her well-worn Bible from the side table. Flipping it open, I searched for her favorite passage. "It's all right, Grandmama. I'm going to read from the Good Book."

"She's been like this for hours now," Grandaddy said. He was standing behind her, pain and fear in his eyes.

It was impossible not to notice that every inch of the margins of Grandmama's Bible were filled with notes, with different colors underlining specific sections. She'd read this Bible hundreds of times over the years.

I turned to her. "I'm going to read your favorite scripture now," I said.

As I sat back and began to read Psalm 23, I was too afraid to look up. *Please, God, not yet!* I prayed. I wanted another day. I needed another day.

"The LORD is my shepherd . . ." My voice shook as I read the first line. "I lack nothing. He makes me lie down in green pastures, he leads me beside quiet waters, he refreshes my soul."

Grandaddy placed his hand on Grandmama's shoulder.

"He guides me along the right paths for his name's sake. Even though I walk through the darkest valley, I will fear no evil, for you are with me; your rod and your staff, they comfort me."

Still not able to meet Grandmama's eyes, I kept on, my voice tight. "You prepare a table before me in the presence of my enemies. You anoint my head with oil, my cup overflows. Surely your goodness and love will follow me all the days of my life, and I will dwell in the house of the LORD forever."

As I finished the psalm, I closed the Bible and looked up at Grandmama. She was watching me with keen eyes and a smile painting her face.

"That's a good word, right there, Timmy." Grandmama leaned forward and touched my cheek. "How are you, my boy?"

I scrubbed at fresh tears as Grandaddy knelt and placed his arms around her.

"There she is," he whispered in her ear. "There's my girl."

Grandmama squeezed Grandaddy's hand as she turned and kissed him on the cheek.

Over the next hour or so we talked, but I honestly can't remember what we talked about. I think it was just normal life stuff. Still, it was magnificent. I often close my eyes and picture that moment. The sun streaming through the window, landing on Grandmama's hands.

After a while, I stopped talking and started listening. For a time at least, she was herself once again. Throughout her life, Grandmama was the most vivacious, charismatic, thoughtful person I've ever known. She was stronger than all of us.

As I watched my grandparents, I didn't want to miss a moment. I watched in wonder as they laughed and told stories. I listened as Grandmama asked about her friends and neighbors. She loved everyone and championed them whether they wanted her to or not. It was a good day. A very good day. It was also the last time I was able to bring Grandmama back for any real amount of time.

Grandmama had Alzheimer's. Over the first few years, it progressed so slowly that we all hoped she had been misdiagnosed. But when the symptoms finally started to manifest, the progression of the disease was stunning.

The next few years were beyond miserable. Honestly, I struggle to make myself remember. Over time, it seemed as if Grandmama had become trapped in her body. She lost the ability to speak and feed herself, to bathe herself. She lived for five years in this state of helplessness.

While my mom, my aunt, and I helped out, it was Grandaddy who was truly there for her. For most of their life, she had taken care of him. Grandmama did the dishes, she cleaned, she cooked, she did the laundry, and she helped in the garden. She did all these things after walking more than a mile home from her full-time job of cleaning houses. To watch Grandaddy step up to the plate and take care of her was amazing.

I wanted to help in a meaningful way, but I'd just started a business and didn't have much money. Together, we took out a high-interest loan of almost $10,000 so Grandaddy could make the house work better for her needs. He installed a contraption in the ceilings that helped move Grandmama from one place to another. He also built a chain in the bathtub to help her get in and out. He was always thinking up new ways to make Grandmama more comfortable.

To say this was a hard time for everyone is the understatement of the century. I don't cry easily, but in this season of life, tears were my frequent companion.

Louida Ware, my grandmother, died on April 29, 2001. It was devastating for us all, but for Grandaddy, it was world-shattering. I know I spoke at the funeral because Mom tells me I did, but I have no memory of it. The entire day has been exiled to the deep recesses of my mind. When I think about that day, I recall only a sequence of images.

The most powerful of those images is Grandaddy sitting, with tears streaming down his face. In all my life, I'd never seen him shed a tear over anything. Watching this powerful and often unyielding man give way to emotion told me everything I needed to know about how he felt about Grandmama.

When I think about my relationship with Grandmama and those last few years, I honestly don't have a single regret. I sat with her twice a week, holding her hand, feeding her, and cleaning her up. Though this is a hard memory, I am proud of how our family banded together.

Today, I am the ranking member of the Senate Special Committee on Aging. This is a position I covet. There are currently 5.7 million people living in the United States with Alzheimer's. This number is expected to triple by 2050. Because of the way it affects the body and mind, and because it often plays out over many years, Alzheimer's is without a doubt the most expensive disease in the nation. This is unacceptable in a country such as ours.

I believe the most powerful people on earth are the people we take for granted the most. Our world rewards physical strength, beauty, and youth. And while I am continuously inspired by the younger generations, wisdom can be gained only through life experience and the passage of time.

We must embrace the truth that the most valuable things in life are free. If there are relationships that need mending, don't wait another minute! We must love one another with abandon. This is who we were created to be.

I am a sitting US senator with more on my plate than ever before, but I still call my mother every day, without fail. We don't usually talk for long. Often I just tell her I love her, and she prays for me and tells me she loves me. I need her in my life. She is wise, courageous, and kind beyond words. I want to be like her when I grow up!

How many of us are here today because of praying grandparents? How many hundreds of hours did they invest in interceding for our health and success or advocating for the success and safety of our kids and our grandkids? They are not just valuable members of our society; they are the reason we are here. And they still have much to give if we simply take the time to listen.

In a world hit hard by COVID-19 and polarized by politics, too many families are at odds with one another. Too many lifelong friends no longer speak to one another. These are ridiculous reasons to be separated from our loved ones. Our relationships are infinitely more powerful than politics! We absolutely must do all in our power to honor and love even those who vehemently disagree with us.

No job on earth should get in the way of the most powerful relationships in our lives. No belief on earth—political or religious—should come between you and your loved ones. Make it a priority to connect with the people who love you most. When we all eventually arrive at the end of our lives, the worst regret is the one that can be the most easily reversed. Spend more time with the people you love. Don't waste another day!

2008

A HISTORIC MOMENT

Grandaddy was dressed in his Sunday best. I didn't think about his clothes when he climbed into my car, but it surely wasn't Sunday. He was silent for a long time as we drove, which wasn't unusual. But something felt different about this silence. Grandaddy was rarely, if ever, anxious about anything in his life, and I rarely saw him excited. That day, I think he might have been filled with both of those emotions.

Grandaddy couldn't help himself from leaning forward during the entire drive. It was almost as if he were trying to add his momentum to the car so we might get there faster.

"You feeling okay?" I asked as we made our way down the road.

There was no response.

"Grandaddy!"

He shook his head and looked at me. "What was that?" he asked. There was a clear look of anticipation in his eyes.

"I asked if you're feeling okay."

"Oh. Mm-hmm," he said. "Yes."

I waited, but nothing more came. Grandaddy wasn't the type of person you pushed for anything. If there was something he didn't want to talk about, nothing in heaven or on earth was going to make him open his mouth. Still clueless about what was happening, I decided to leave well enough alone and just drive.

When we arrived, Grandaddy took a long, slow breath before exiting the car. He stood for a moment, using his reflection in the car window to adjust his cap. I waited until he turned to me.

"Okay," he said. "I'm ready."

We walked together and stood in a line that stretched two and a half blocks. It was when we joined the line that I became aware of the feeling of expectation vibrating from almost everyone around us. To be honest, I still didn't get it. I hadn't taken the time to think about the power of the moment we were living in from Grandaddy's perspective. A black man born in segregated times was now participating in the election that could result in the first black president.

When we finally got to the front of the line, a volunteer

recognized me. She knew exactly who I was and what I stood for. And by the look in her eyes, she was not a fan. She turned to Grandaddy.

"Sir, you can go to the open booth right over there." She pointed as she placed a hand on his shoulder.

"I need help," Grandaddy said with a smile. "I asked my grandson Timmy to help me out."

The lady looked at me, clearly skeptical. "Are you sure, sir?"

"Of course, I'm sure!" Grandaddy said as he began walking toward the booth.

As I followed close behind, the woman stared daggers at me. She didn't think I would honor my grandaddy's choice and seemed certain I was about to steal his vote.

We stood for a long moment and stared at the screen together. Grandaddy couldn't read a word, so I pointed to the name. I knew he would see the name on the news and in the papers, and his memory was picture-perfect. Once he learned what the name looked like, he would be able to pick it out anywhere.

"Barack Obama," I said as I pointed to the name.

With a shaking hand, he reached out and pressed the button. After pressing it, he just stared at the screen with a look of wonder in his eyes.

I was also on the ballot that year in another state house district. But Grandaddy didn't live in my district, so he couldn't vote for me, although he was sure to tell me how desperately proud he was. In that moment, it was the experience of voting for a black man to become the leader of the free world that moved him to his core.

As we drove away, I looked over at Grandaddy, and for the second and last time in my life, I saw tears streaming down his face.

I was on the county council back then, and I'd just become the chairman a few months earlier. Though I experienced moments of racism and even hatred, I didn't grow up being treated like three-fifths of a man.[3] Whatever struggles I may have experienced, they didn't hold a candle to those of my grandaddy, Artis Ware.

I always knew the magnitude of the 2008 presidential election. I fully understood the gravity of the moment. Ultimately, I saw this race as a philosophical choice. It was the steel will of my grandaddy that helped me to grasp the full weight of history as experienced through a person who for too long hadn't been seen or accepted in the country he helped build.

As I watched Grandaddy process the moment, I took the time to appreciate it as well. My grandaddy had lived long enough to see someone who looked like him run for the highest office in the land. As I drove him back home, Grandaddy talked more than I ever remember him talking. He was excited. He was animated.

"Timmy, the miracle isn't whether he wins or not. The miracle is that he is on the ballot!"

The story of black America, especially for Grandaddy's generation, was having someone in the room. For most of our history, black America didn't have that kind of influence or power. There was no such position for someone who looked like us. At the very best, there might have been a black man or woman behind the scenes, in the room where the decisions were being made.

For Grandaddy, the idea that a black man isn't merely in the room but at the top of the ticket was simply unbelievable. The fact that this black man from the Midwest had beaten the Clintons—the establishment icons—was impossible!

"Timmy, for more than half of my life I wasn't allowed to vote." Grandaddy had a faraway look in his eyes. "I know you may not like what this man stands for, but hear me when I tell you," he said, choking back tears, "win or lose, this is a great day for our country."

As we drove home, I saw Grandaddy through a new set of eyes. Not only did he help illuminate the importance of that moment in our history, but the experience taught me a critical life lesson.

Like many, I struggled with countless moments of President Obama's eight years. While I believe him to be a brilliant speaker and a great father and husband who wants the best for our country, we are diametrically opposed in our beliefs about what policies will get us there. Still, I can—and did—celebrate what his election meant for our country.

It is easy to champion someone who thinks and looks like us. But I believe the power to change hearts and minds will only come through opening our own hearts and minds. Rather than throw stones at those who disagree with us or become angry and aggressive toward those who think differently, try listening. Civility leads to compassion, and compassion gives us the courage to press on.

Call your mother. Call your brother. But also call your neighbor who doesn't look or think like you. Create some space for a relationship that transcends politics or religion. Only when we, as a nation, can put people above politics will we see the change we so ardently desire.

NINE

THREE GENERATIONS

1919

The sweat pouring down Isaac Doctor's face had little to do with the Charleston heat. Running faster than he had ever run in his life, Isaac's lungs burned—but he kept on. *Stupid! Stupid! Stupid!* The thought thundered through his head. *Why didn't you just move?*

The shouts of the pursuing men were closer now. As he darted into an alley, Isaac ran headlong into a woman carrying a basket of laundry, sending them both to the muddied ground in a heap.

"I'm sorry!" he said. The words came out in a terrified wheeze as he leaped to his feet. But before he could take three steps, the men were on him. They threw him face-first to the ground, and as the first boot landed, Isaac could feel his ribs snap. The woman watched in horror while five sailors brutally murdered Isaac Doctor simply because the black man had refused to move aside to let the white men pass him on the sidewalk.

Although the full story is unclear, and there are many

differing stories of exactly what incident sparked the riot of 1919 in Charleston, South Carolina, what is known is that Isaac's death was one of the embers. More than a thousand white sailors from the nearby navy yard wreaked havoc on the city. They attacked black individuals, businesses, and homes. They pulled down trolley poles and brutalized the black men and women inside the trolley cars. Many African American men and women died that night.

This was a dark time for America.

This was an unjust time in America.

———

Two years later, in 1921, in the rural town of Salley, not far from the spot where Isaac Doctor was killed, Artis Ware was born. This is the world into which my grandaddy was born.

Grandaddy lived at a time in which, for all intents and purposes, he had no rights. He could have been shot, hanged, or beaten with impunity. My grandaddy was a man who would step off the sidewalk when white people walked his way. The story of Isaac Doctor was something he learned early in life.

My grandaddy lived under the specter of racism his entire life. He lived under a system that had been designed for his oppression. He knew it. Everybody knew it. And those in power wanted to make it clear that my grandaddy was still just three-fifths of a man.

If I've ever known a man who had the right to be bitter, it was Grandaddy. Yet I never once saw bitterness in him. Instead, he provided for his family, served his community, and—along with my grandmama—raised a strong, powerful black woman to be proud of who she was and where she came from.

1955

A TIME OF TRANSITION

Eight years in and the magic of walking to the plate hadn't faded a bit. Jackie Robinson loved everything about the game. The smell of the grass. The smooth wood in his hands. The hard stare of the opposing pitcher. This was where he was meant to be. This was home.

As the youngest of five brothers, Jackie always had to be tough. While they were all close, his brother Mack set the standard. At the 1936 Summer Olympics, he won the silver medal in the 200 meters, finishing behind Jesse Owens. Mack reminded Jackie regularly that he had never beaten him. Jackie was still chasing a win against his brother.

As Jackie stepped to the plate, something shifted. Feeling as if he were in a dream, he couldn't help but smile. The world slowed down around him, and he knew he was about to do something magical. He closed his eyes. He breathed deeply as he envisioned himself swinging. In his mind's eye, he could see the bat connect and the ball explode as if shot from a cannon.

A fastball flies up to 100 miles per hour. The ball travels 60 feet 6 inches before it reaches the bat. That gives a batter four-tenths of a second to react. Jackie ran through the numbers, a ritual he repeated every time he walked up to the plate.

In a game of split-second decisions, the smallest hesitation means the difference between being one of the best players on earth and just another guy in the local beer league. You must trust your gut. You must trust your instinct. And then you must go all out, as if your life depended on it. Every time Jackie Robinson stood at home plate, every time he waited on a base, he went all out.

Jackie lifted the bat to his shoulder as he met the pitcher's eyes. Over the years, this had become one of his favorite moments. Every now and again he could see their fear, as he did at that moment. His smile deepened. This pitcher knew exactly who he was facing.

That night set the Brooklyn Dodgers on a path to winning their first World Series. Jackie Robinson hit a home run and stole a base—home base. It was a team victory, but Jackie was the hero.

Jackie was the first African American to play in Major League Baseball. He was a true civil rights champion, but he found it almost humorous that history would remember him because of the color of his skin. He was the best because he worked harder than anyone else and pushed himself past the breaking point every single day. He was the best because he gave everything he had to the game. Why should the color of his skin matter?

————

Three years before Jackie Robinson first set foot on a Major League Baseball field, Frances Ware was born. This is the world my mother was born into.

Mom lived during a time of transition. She was ten years old when *Brown v. Board of Education of Topeka* (1954) ruled that segregation in the public schools was unconstitutional. One year later, she listened to the radio in awe as the newscasters told the story of true-life hero Rosa Parks.

Throughout the 1950s and 1960s, it was almost as if a mirror were held up to the face of our nation—and we did not like what we saw. Though it was painful and there were many setbacks, my mother's generation brought about unbelievable progress on the issues of race and inequality.

1978

A RACE RIOT

The location for the fight wasn't the most well thought out. Just a few steps outside of the principal's office, the two young men were in an all-out, old-fashioned fistfight. Byron's left eye was already swollen, and Reggie's nose was dripping blood. In the hallway, at least twenty students had gathered to cheer on one side or the other.

Byron ducked and Reggie's fist missed its mark. Charging, Reggie slammed into Byron. He lifted Byron high and hurled him onto the ground, landing on top of him. He was only able to get a couple of good punches in before two teachers pulled him off. Suddenly everyone in the hallway found the pressing need to be somewhere else as both young men were escorted to the principal's office.

Byron was a self-proclaimed redneck. In fact, he was a member of a gang that called themselves the Rednecks. You could tell who was in the gang by the cuffs on their blue jeans and their upturned short sleeves.

Reggie was black, and his brother was a well-known member of the competing Ten Mile Hill Gang, which got its name from the neighborhood where most of its members lived. Ten Miles is a stretch of road in Charleston. In 1979, this was a predominantly black and impoverished neighborhood.

The Ten Mile Hill Gang were all students at Stall High School, and many were on the football team. Whenever the Rednecks or some other group threatened a black kid, its members stepped in—self-styled regulators as if the school were the Wild West.

In the parking lot after school, Byron bragged to anyone who would listen, "I got me one. I got me a nigger."

News of the fight and Byron's words spread quickly. "You could feel it in the air," a student told the police the following day. "Everyone was talking about it. There was going to be a riot."

The following morning, every member of the Rednecks was gathered in the parking lot. For the most part, they all owned their own vehicles or had their parents drop them off. They had arrived early with hopes of intimidating every black kid who entered the school. There were at least fifty of them.

As they waited, Byron thought he heard something. Slowly, every member of the Rednecks turned to watch as two buses pulled into the parking lot.

Inside the buses was every member of the Ten Mile Hill Gang, including some who had graduated from Stall High School a year or two earlier. And every person inside the buses was ready to fight.

The closer the buses came, the clearer the chanting became. Every kid on the bus was shouting at the top of his lungs, "Let the competition beware! Let the competition beware! Let the competition beware!"

The moment the bus doors opened, anger erupted. There were fights everywhere. These weren't your typical posturing high school altercations. In every direction, scores of young men engaged in all-out brawls.

It didn't take the police long to arrive. At least ten squad cars came screeching in, bringing the fights to an abrupt end.

Everyone was sent home. There would be no school that day.

———

A year after the fight between the Rednecks and the Ten Mile Hill Gang, a student named Tim Scott entered Stall High School as a freshman. And just three years later, the students were asked to choose between a young Filipino woman and a young black man to lead them as their student government president.

These very same students elected me. This is the world I grew up in.

2015

PLEASE REMIND THEM OF ROMANS 8:28

My hands have hovered over the keys of my laptop for almost an hour. I had planned to share the story of Mother Emanuel just as I told the stories of Isaac Doctor, Jackie Robinson, and the race riot in my high school. Yet I haven't been able to write a single word.

I'd planned to paint a picture, to put you inside the South Carolina church where men and women gathered to study the Bible together. I wanted you to feel the love these true-life saints were pouring into each other. I wanted you to hear their fervent prayers to God for the health of their loved ones, their community, and their nation, and that they may be shining lights in the midst of darkness. I wanted you to see them as they truly were: the best among us. I wanted to do this because they deserve it.

But as I sat in front of my computer, I could not even begin. I didn't know how. I have pictured the scene a thousand times. And every time it cut me to the core more than anything I have ever experienced.

On June 17, 2015, a man whose name I shall never utter was welcomed into Mother Emanuel AME Church and loved on by its members. He was invited to join them in reading the Bible, praying, and encouraging one another. Then he retrieved a weapon with the singular goal of extinguishing those shining lights.

On that day, nine saints were murdered: Daniel L. Simmons Sr., Clementa C. Pinckney, Cynthia Graham Hurd, Susie Jackson, Ethel Lee Lance, Depayne Middleton-Doctor, Tywanza Sanders, Sharonda Coleman-Singleton, and Myra Thompson. They were some of the best people our country had to offer.

A week or so after the massacre, I was in Washington and moments away from walking onto the Senate floor. I was there to deliver a speech about the atrocity when I felt the need to make a call. I had reached out to the families of the nine saints, but I had yet to speak to all of them.

The phone rang three times before Daniel Simmons Jr. picked it up.

"Hello, this is Daniel."

"Daniel, I'm so glad to hear your voice. This is Tim Scott, and I have been wanting to speak with you. Do you have a couple of minutes?"

"Yes. Sure. Thanks for calling."

"Daniel, I want you to know my heart is broken over the loss of your father and the others. I have been praying for you all daily, and if there is anything I can do, all you need to do is ask."

"That means a lot. Thank you very much."

"Listen, Daniel. I am about to speak to the US Senate about what happened, and I want to know if there is anything you want me to tell them. What would you like me to say about the loss of your father and the other saints? Whatever it is, you have my word, I will be your voice today."

There was a long silence before he answered. I was expecting something heavy and dark and painful, but it wasn't. Frankly, what Daniel said stunned me.

"Please remind them of Romans 8:28: 'And we know that in

all things God works for the good of those who love him, who have been called according to his purpose.'"

This time I was the one who was silent.

Daniel continued, "I don't know how, but I am certain we can count on the fact that God is going to use what happened in an amazing way."

This is what faith looks like. The thought came to me unbidden. I sat there with the phone in my hand, choked up and momentarily unable to speak.

His father, Daniel Sr., had been executed in his church, and somehow Daniel was certain God was going to turn this loss into an even greater good.

I need to tell the story of the Emanuel Nine because I know some may read this chapter and believe I have my head in the sand. Make no mistake. I am intimately familiar with the scars our nation bears. Racism is a reality in America, but I know that many of us are doing our all-out best to extinguish it. I am proud to live in a country and among people who have spent the last hundred-plus years examining our systems, the legal structures we hold so dear, and uprooting systemic racism.

I will shout from the rooftops that the US justice system isn't yet fully just. Far too many black Americans are treated poorly by law enforcement. Far too many brown Americans are unfairly targeted because of the color of their skin. Far too many lower-income Americans are sentenced more harshly than their affluent counterparts. I've spent much of my time in political office fighting to bring justice to these very real issues.

I have written two different books and spoken on many occasions about the more than twenty instances I've been pulled over for DWB (driving while black). In those moments I felt every emotion you might imagine: humiliated, angry, belittled.

I understand we, as a nation, have miles to go before we rest. Yet while bitterness may be the easy choice, redemption is where the power lies. And I will choose redemption every time.

There are two ways to view history. One is to shine an unwavering light on the myriad atrocities that have befallen us. And there is nothing wrong with having a realistic and honest accounting of history. In fact, it's vital that we do so. It helps to keep us from repeating it.

From my experience, however, dwelling on the pain of the past for too long threatens to keep us mired there. When I look back, I prefer to focus on how far we've come. Only then can I envision how beautiful the road ahead could be. It is that vision that motivates me to fight to my last breath to get us there.

I know the anger I see throughout our country. The brutal murder of George Floyd captured live on multiple cameras shook this nation to its very foundation. There is real darkness in this world, but it is in the midst of this darkness that the light shines brightest. We are that light. You and I were created for such a time as this.

When I look at my heritage, I don't see a single person in my family through the eyes of pain or loss, and I have never seen anyone as a victim. I see my family as champions who played a role in creating a bold and bright new future. I see them as heroes who pushed our country in the right direction. I believe they and so many others sowed blood, tears, and greatness into the fabric of our nation, and today we are reaping the harvest.

I often conflate the words *hope* and *redemption*. While I understand they are different, I also believe they are inexorably linked. More than any other words in the English language, these two words define me. I view our history, our present, and our future through the twin lenses of hope and redemption. Sometimes you have to look a little harder to see them.

I view our last fifty years as miracle upon miracle. We are absolutely a nation striving toward redemption. Our story is moving in the right direction, and we are moving swiftly. I choose hope. I choose to believe in a story of redemption. This is the only real choice we have. In my family alone, I can point to three generations, each experiencing the world from a drastically different place. I am proud to be in this fight. I am proud to have my story play a role in the greater story of ultimate redemption.

Hope.

Redemption.

This is your story.

This is our story as a nation.

Embrace it. Believe it. Pray for it. Then live it. Every single day. Believe your story matters. Believe you are here to make this country and this world a better place.

TEN

HAIL TO THE CHIEF

2008

Of all the years to walk away from a successful career and try to reinvent yourself, 2008 was quite possibly the worst choice.

What am I going to do? This thought pounded through Jennifer DeCasper's head dozens of times each day. Jac sat on the floor in front of her, playing with her multicolored stacking rings. Jac, short for Jacoby, was one year old and completely clueless about the dark place her mother was in.

I am a failure and everyone knows it. Jennifer struggled to find a deep breath as she stared at her daughter. "What am I going to do?" she whispered.

"What was that, honey?" her mom asked as she entered the living room.

"Nothing. I was just . . . nothing."

Jennifer's mom sat on the couch beside her. "You know we don't mind you living here," she said carefully. "We are happy to help however we can. But are you sure you don't want to go back?"

Some version of this conversation happened on a weekly basis. Jennifer knew her parents wanted the best for her, but she had been living with them for a year now.

"I'm sure, Mom," she said. "I don't know how to explain it, but this is where I am meant to be." She let out a tight breath. She felt brittle as she scooped up her daughter. "I need to get Jac to day care or I'll be late for work."

Jennifer gathered her daughter's things and walked out of her parents' house feeling like an absolute failure. *Single mom. Failed career. Living with my parents. Very little savings. I can't even afford a car.* These and other thoughts pounded through her head as she buckled Jac into the back of her sister's car.

Trying to keep the dark thoughts at bay, Jennifer played gospel singer Marvin Sapp as she drove. In between songs, she broke down in tears. "I am not a failure," she whispered as Jac sang along in the back seat.

Drop-off should have been quick, but Jennifer struggled to leave her daughter. She held her close, hugging her for a very long time before finally breaking away. By the time she pulled up to the airport, her eyes were red and puffy. Quickly checking her reflection in the rearview mirror, she tried her best to calm down. *Okay, time to go to work.*

Landing the job at the airport had required her to be creative on her résumé. Her boss and colleagues had no idea she had graduated from the University of Michigan Law School with a juris doctorate. None of her colleagues had a clue she had worked as a deputy district attorney in Colorado for a couple of years. It had been a good life. She'd had a great reputation with the judges and the defense attorneys, and she loved the idea that she was making her community safer and better. Yet, as the years passed, it was the idea of working on Capitol Hill, making a difference by influencing the policies that affected the lives of *every* American, that kept her awake at night.

The move from Colorado to Washington, DC, had been bold. The drive across the country had been filled with hope and purpose. Some of her friends thought she'd lost her mind. "You are thinking selfishly. You are a mom now. You need to think about what's best for Jac," they told her.

On that drive she had determined to prove them wrong. But as Jennifer walked onto the runway with glow sticks in her hands, wearing a fluorescent vest, it was hard not to agree with them. More than anything, what she felt was an overwhelming sense of shame. She believed she was meant to do something great. She believed the move to Washington was something she was meant to do. If that were true, however, why was absolutely nothing working? The acrid smell of jet fuel filled her nostrils as she waved her glow sticks, directing the plane out onto the runway.

Jennifer in fact had two full-time jobs: working at the airport and applying for jobs on the Hill. Every night, after she put Jac to bed, Jennifer spent hours searching and applying for jobs. At first she'd been incredibly confident. She applied to only the best opportunities, the positions for which she was best suited, the ones that felt the most exciting. But after a year, she began to throw her résumé at any position—on or off the Hill—that was hiring.

On this particular day, her shift ended early. As she climbed back into her sister's car to drive home, Jennifer felt a familiar vibration in her pocket. She retrieved her phone and answered it.

"Hello."

"Hello, is this Jennifer DeCasper?"

"Yes, this is Jennifer."

"Joe McKeown here. I'm with Congressman-elect Tim Scott.

I'm wondering if you can come to DC this afternoon for an interview. Someone handed me your résumé a few days back. I honestly didn't know people still had paper résumés, but I suppose it works just as well. Anyway, I think you might be a good fit for our policy shop."

"Of course. Yes. I will absolutely make it. What time do I need to be there?"

After she hung up, Jennifer realized she had no idea what the job was. Yet, in this moment, she didn't care. There wasn't enough time to go back to her parents' house to change into something appropriate for the interview, so she drove to the nearest Target.

She darted between the racks. *Too loud. Too low-cut. Screams unprofessional.* These thoughts raced through her mind as she searched the racks. *I need something that says, "This woman is professional, brilliant, hardworking, and dedicated."*

The perfect outfit didn't materialize, and she instead landed on what was available. It would have to do.

As she parked outside the office, Jennifer searched the surrounding area. When she saw no one in sight, she quickly changed in the car. Feeling flustered yet hopeful, she walked toward the first real job interview she'd had in a year.

She was directed to the conference room, and as she entered she introduced herself to the man sitting at the table. "Hello, I'm here for the interview," she said. "Joe McKeown called me earlier today."

"That's right, I'm Joe. Thanks for making it down on such short notice," he said as he offered his hand.

"Of course," Jennifer said. "Not a problem at all."

"Congressman-elect Scott is finishing up another meeting, but he should be free any minute now. Just have a seat."

Jennifer sat down and took out her phone. Over the next few

minutes, she looked up every article she could find on US Senator Tim Scott. There wasn't much information available, but what she read, she liked. *Wow, I think I really want this job.*

The next part of this story, Jennifer and I remember differently. To be fair, I am certain her memory is correct. I just don't love how I am portrayed in the meeting, so I choose to remember it differently. I asked Jennifer to write this next bit. To be clear, what follows is her side of the story.

OLD-SCHOOL, KID-N-PLAY, CABBAGE-PATCH SHUFFLE

The first time I met Tim Scott, it was brutal. I mean, it was a "let me please die in peace now" moment. I have interviewed for numerous jobs over the years, and I am quite proficient at it. It's one of the places where I shine. Unfortunately, that day, I literally had the worst interview of my life.

Over the last couple of pages, Tim had painted an accurate picture of my life. I'd hit what I thought was rock bottom, and I had been living there for a while. My emotional stability was wavering, and my confidence was tested daily.

Tim, on the other hand, had just been elected to Congress, and though he had copious experience as a county councilman and a state house representative in Charleston, he had no idea what he was about to face in Washington.

What Tim didn't tell you is that before I worked as a deputy district attorney in Colorado, I'd worked as a scheduler for my home state senator, Wayne Allard, in his DC office. Although I left the Hill in an administrative function, I knew I was qualified to work as a policy staffer. I merely needed to convince Tim of this fact. And, in that moment, I believed my chic Target attire and I were going to do just that.

Because he was still congressman-elect, Tim didn't have an office. He was conducting all his interviews in a DC hotel ballroom. When I walked in, Tim stood and greeted me. "Hey, you must be Jennifer. Thanks for making it in." Joe McKeown followed me in from the conference room just outside and took a seat beside Tim.

"Of course. Yes. Thank you for the opportunity."

"I have to be honest," Tim said as he took a seat. "I looked through your résumé, and I'm not quite sure why we are meeting."

Welp. There went my great start. "I think if you look at my experience as a district attorney—"

"It says you're from Colorado. Have you ever spent any time down south?"

"Absolutely. Yes. I've been to Miami a couple of times."

"I'm sorry. What?" Tim and Joe shared a look I didn't quite understand.

"I've been to . . . Miami?" I hesitated as an amused look entered Tim's eyes. In my defense, Miami is *technically* south of Washington, DC.

Tim couldn't help himself. He laughed. He didn't intend to be mean. He simply couldn't stop his authentic reaction.

I have a decent sense of humor and thick skin. But on that day, looking up at the world from rock bottom, Tim's laughter felt cruel.

He could see I was upset, and he immediately apologized. "I'm sorry. I really shouldn't have laughed. It's just that Miami isn't really 'south' in the way I mean it." Tim continued scanning my résumé. "Have you ever worked for an elected official?"

"Yes, of course," I said. I'd worked for a senator as well as an elected district attorney, so I was ready.

"Well, it says here you were *just* a scheduler."

Oh. At that moment I realized Tim Scott had no real idea how a congressional office was run. I clearly had more knowledge of the roles and organization of a successful congressional office than he did. But how could I help him see it without sounding disrespectful?

"Mr. Scott, a House scheduler is one of the most complicated and integral roles within a successful office." I tried not to sound like a lecturer. "I left an administrative position to go to law school. I also worked for an elected district attorney. I'd like to come back in a policy position. I understand what it means to represent someone whose name is on the door."

"I just don't understand the connection," Tim said. "Working as an attorney is drastically different from what you are applying for."

Every muscle in my body tightened. My poker face was crumbling. My Target shirt was feeling warm. A deep well of frustration and resentment I'd been ignoring for so long was bubbling up inside of me, and I was struggling to hide it.

"Listen," he said, "aside from the *clear* lack of experience, I'm trying to understand your why. Why do you want to be here?"

I could've told him a ton of things. *I want to help people. I want to change the trajectory of people's lives. I want to be a part of real solutions.* But I could tell I would've sounded like every other bright-eyed Hill staffer. Plus, I was feeling desperate, and I couldn't let that come through. There was no way I was going to let that image of me come across.

After waiting a while for my answer, Tim started telling me about his why.

And that's when I lost it. I burst into tears. This wasn't a "subtly wipe the tears away" moment. This was an all-out, loud, ugly cry. The reality of my previous year mixed with the world's worst interview for a job I was realizing I desperately wanted all came crashing down. In that moment I felt bad for Tim and Joe. I imagined myself in their place and considered what I would think if I were them. That didn't help calm me down, because now I was mortified.

"Do you . . . Do you want to talk about . . . it?" Tim asked.

"No," I said, and I stood. "I'd like to end this interview."

Tim looked a little shell-shocked. "Are you sure?"

Joe was a true gentleman and averted his eyes so I wouldn't feel even more embarrassed.

"Absolutely," I said through snorts and sobs as I almost ran out of the room.

The next week of my life was a void. While I thought I'd hit rock bottom before, I'd somehow managed to find a shovel and dig myself even deeper. Then I received another call from Joe.

"Jennifer, how are you doing? Joe here."

"Um, good? Good. Yes. How are you?"

"I'm great. Thanks for asking. Listen, I'm calling because we wanted to offer you the job."

I almost dropped my phone. It was a very short call, but when I hung up, I began to dance. Like an all-out, old-school, kid-n-play, cabbage-patch shuffle. I was going to be a congressional staffer. I could finally say that it was all worth it. The raised eyebrows, the questioning of my decisions, the judgments—it was all worth it!

A year or so after I started working with Tim, I finally asked the question I had wanted to ask since my first day. We were sitting in his office and had just finished a meeting.

"Can I ask you a question?"

"Of course," Tim said.

"Why did you hire me? Because that was the worst interview ever."

This is a family photo celebrating my reelection to the Senate in 2014. From left to right, my cousin's wife Olga, my nephew's mom Mia, my aunt Nita, my cousin Otis, my mom Frances, my niece Kendra and her husband Marcus, my grandaddy, and my nephew Ben.

My mom and me at Bon Secours St. Francis Hospital where she has worked since 1973. This was taken in 2018 when I surprised her with flowers for Valentine's Day.

My mom in 1983;
she was thirty-nine.

My grandparents Artis and Louida in their
living room in North Charleston. If I remember
correctly, this was taken on Christmas morning.

My grandaddy tending his garden in North Charleston.
Gardening was one of his favorite past times.

In 1966 I was one year old. My aunt Nita
has been one of my greatest champions
for as long as I can remember.

My official Midland Park Elementary School picture of 1975. I was ten years old.

My official Stall High School senior picture. This was the year I won the election for student body government president.

My junior year of high school. It was a 1982 touchdown run that I can still remember vividly. It was my favorite year of football by far and just one season before my life-changing car accident.

Taken in 1982, just a year after I first met John Moniz. John was a true mentor who taught me so many things, not least of which was the power of pursuing God-size dreams.

Greg and Kassy Alia on their wedding day in 2015. I never had the honor of meeting Greg, who was a police officer in Richard County South Carolina. Greg was killed in the line of duty on September 30, 2015. Kassy is a force of nature. After Greg's death, she launched www.serveandconnect.org.

Photo by Dave Kugler, Kassy's father.

This is Greg, Kassy, and their son Salvatore Alia. This photo was taken just four months before the loss of Greg.

My friend and brother Brian Moniz. Brian is also the son of my mentor John Moniz. I tell his story in these pages. He is a man of true integrity and one of my oldest friends. Brian is a police officer in Charleston County.

Jennifer DeCasper (my Chief of Staff) and me when we were celebrating a legislative achievement.

Taken at a rally at the North Charleston Coliseu
and Performing Arts Center in 201(

"One hundred percent. Worst. Interview. Ever." Tim laughed at the memory. "Honestly, I went home that night and prayed about it, and I really felt like God was saying you were the right person for the job. I argued with God for a week about it because, well, you get it. You were there."

We both laughed this time.

"But it was clear you were passionate, and passion goes a long way in my book."

I'll let Tim pick up the story from here. I've written enough of his memoir for him already. Before I give the floor back to my boss, though, I want you to know who he is. Tim is a man who champions everyone in his life. Yes, I think he is great at his job. But more than that, he is a great human who loves unconditionally. It might take an outburst of tears, but he sees your heart. He sees your value in your story. He views your journey as a strength. And now when he pokes at me, I just poke back.

Proverbs 27:17 says, "As iron sharpens iron, so one person sharpens another." I've never felt more blessed, proud, or honored to work for someone who allows me to sharpen him as much as he sharpens me. God bless the iron in our lives!

THE POWER OF HITTING ROCK BOTTOM

To be honest, the moment Jennifer fled the interview, I had a pretty strong feeling that she was the one for the job. Even though the interview was arguably horrible, her heart was so clearly good. She oozed compassion and brilliance.

I remember turning to Joe McKeown and asking, "What do you think?"

"I know this may sound insane," he said, "but I really like her."

"Me too," I laughed. "I want to go home and pray about it, but I don't think we should bother interviewing anyone else for now."

Within a year, Jennifer DeCasper was promoted to my deputy chief of staff. And a year after arriving in the Senate, I promoted her to chief of staff. Jennifer tells our staff all the time that if they want to advance in our office, their job description is "filling holes." If there's a need to be addressed, whether it's answering phones, retrieving silverware for an event, or cleaning a stain in the carpet, no matter what you think your job description is, just do it. This has always been her work ethic, and this is one of the many reasons she was promoted so quickly and excels today.

Though I know it was impossibly hard, Jennifer speaks often of how meaningful it was to work at the airport for a year. I guess that experience is at least part of the reason she is so humble. She is a true servant. Though it is unquestionably painful to feel that you are at your wits' end, it is those moments that strip us bare of any remnant of ego or self-importance.

There is something powerful about hitting rock bottom and finding your way back up. Once you have been there, you don't fear it anymore. Jennifer is fearless. Speak with anyone on Capitol Hill, and you will quickly learn that she is universally respected as one of the best chiefs of staff there is. She has shattered the stereotype that a single mom can't also be incredibly successful. Her daughter, Jac, is a member of my family. Jac spent half the pandemic attending school virtually out of our conference room.

If I had looked at Jennifer's interview at face value, I would quickly have moved on to another candidate. But I believe everyone I meet is in the midst of a battle I can't fully understand. In the week I wrote this chapter, we have witnessed the botched withdrawal from Afghanistan, we've seen an earthquake hit Haiti, we've experienced a hurricane strike the Gulf Coast. As a nation, we are fighting many battles on many fronts. And as individuals, they are amplified tenfold because of the repercussions on our mental health.

According to the Centers for Disease Control and Prevention (CDC), 41.5 percent of American adults are experiencing anxiety or depression, 71 percent of Americans are angry, and 66 percent of us are fearful.[4] And that's just adults. In many ways, I think our children are feeling it even more. A 2017 report showed that the depression rate among twelve- to seventeen-year-olds in the past decade had doubled—a troubling trend that has continued in the years since.[5]

I read a *New York Times* article titled "There's a Name for the Blah You're Feeling: It's Called Languishing."[6] In psychology, mental health has a scale from flourishing to depression. Flourishing is evidenced by things such as optimism, empathy, authenticity, inner joy, strong self-esteem, and a sense of meaning. On the other side of that spectrum is depression. This is evidenced by feelings such as hopelessness and helplessness, sensing that the best is behind you.

It doesn't matter where you are on the mental health scale, there is a way up and a way out. No matter how dark or how hard things may be, there is light at the end of the tunnel. Jennifer's story is my story. Her story is your story.

While I believe policy matters (a lot!), I know that valuing people matters a whole lot more. I care far more about the Creator in whose image you are made than your political affiliation. While my colleagues on the other side of the aisle may approach the world through a different lens, they were made by the same God who made me—and you.

As we come out of the pandemic, the emotional health of our nation needs far more attention. Too many of our kids are depressed. Suicide attempts are at an all-time high. I don't believe government is the answer, or I should say I believe government is merely a small part of the answer.

We live in a day and age that hasn't merely picked sides; it asks us to dig trenches. Rather than endeavoring to understand or start a dialogue, we are told to throw bombs. I believe it is this "us or them" mindset that feeds the feelings of anxiety and depression that underlie our collective and individual experiences. If every day is a battle on every front, where can we find reprieve?

I choose to love people and champion them irrespective of their beliefs. I think what's missing in our culture and society today is that we no longer embrace people who look or sound different from us. We are encouraged to stay huddled in our protective circles of people who think, look, and react as we do, like our high school cliques.

In a culture that thrives on tearing down, I choose to build people up. Whether I meet you on your worst day or your best day, you are going to find the same version of me. Like Jennifer DeCasper, Americans have an uncanny ability to persevere, to work through pain. There will always be dark times ahead, but I choose to focus on the beauty, wonder, and magic of the world around me.

I believe our best days as a country are ahead of us. But what's more important—and hear me when I say this—I believe no matter where you find yourself today, there are great things in store for *you*. Don't give up. No matter how dark the world may appear, I promise you, redemption is close at hand.

ELEVEN

PRESIDENT TRUMP

2018

My mother and I were driving to her seventy-fifth birthday party. She was wearing a beautiful dress and didn't look a day over sixty. She thought we were getting together with eight or nine friends for a low-key party. But in reality, more than a hundred people whose lives my mother had influenced in some way were waiting to surprise her.

For this very auspicious occasion, I'd gone all out. Bishop T. D. Jakes and hometown country star Darius Rucker, who is also the lead singer of the awesome band Hootie and the Blowfish, had sent video messages wishing my mother a happy birthday. Many of her closest friends had also created videos, and we'd stitched them into a compilation. I was excited to celebrate my mother's life, but I was also slightly disappointed because the video I had been anxiously waiting for hadn't arrived.

When we were fifteen minutes from our destination, my phone rang.

"Hello?"

"Is this Senator Scott?"

"Yes."

"Please hold for the president of the United States," the voice said.

"Of course. Yes," I said as a smile parted my lips. I was relatively certain the president wasn't calling me to talk policy. A moment later, President Donald Trump was on the other side of the call.

"Tim, how are you?"

"I'm well, Mr. President. Thanks for asking. How are you, sir?"

"Fantastic. Couldn't be better, thanks," he said. "Now listen, I hear today's a special day for someone you love."

"Yes, it is, Mr. President. That's right. Today is my mother's seventy-fifth birthday."

"Seventy-five! Good for her! That's great. Just great. Is she with you? I'd love to wish her a happy birthday. Would that be all right?"

"Yes, sir. She is right here. I'll hand over the phone."

I held the phone out to my mom. "Mom, the president of the United States would like to speak with you."

"What?!" A combination of shock and disbelief reflected in my mom's eyes.

"Mom, you need to take the phone," I prompted as I raised an eyebrow. "It's not really polite to keep the president waiting."

My mom grabbed the phone with a skeptical look in her eyes. I'll never forget the moment she placed the phone to her ear. Watching her confusion shift to surprise and then to pure delight might be one of my favorite memories.

A month or so earlier, I'd been at the White House for a

meeting and had run into Mick Mulvaney, President Trump's chief of staff at the time. Mick was also a former South Carolina congressman, so we had a relationship that spanned a number of years. On a whim, I pulled him aside and asked if there was any way the president might be able to send a card or a video message for my mom's seventy-fifth birthday.

Mick thought about it for a moment. "No promises, but I'll give it a shot," he said.

"I would certainly appreciate it. I know it would mean the world to her."

"Oh, my God! Oh, my God! Oh, my God!" my mother kept saying over and over into the phone.

Finally, I had to step in. "Mom, we get it. You're excited. Now how about you and President Trump talk for a moment."

"Right, yes. Mr. President, thank you so much for calling. Oh, my God!" My mom finally settled down, and I listened as she and President Trump talked for the entire drive, probably fifteen minutes.

She handed the phone back to me. "Tim, you are one lucky man to have such an incredible mama."

"I couldn't agree more, sir."

"Listen, if there is anything you need from me, ever, just say the word, and I'll make it happen."

"I appreciate that, Mr. President. And thank you so much for calling."

"Of course. The pleasure was all mine. You have a great rest of your night, okay?"

"Thank you, Mr. President. You as well."

When my mother exited the car, she was glowing. When she entered the room to find so many friends waiting, she could hardly believe it.

My mama is no bragger and is without a doubt the humblest and most godly woman I have ever known. But as the night wore on, she managed to find a way to tell every one of her friends about the call she'd received from the president of the United States.

———

A month or so later, I was back in the White House on official business. On my way out, President Trump pulled me aside. "Listen, I really enjoyed speaking with your mom. That was really a lot of fun. She is clearly one amazing woman," he said as we walked together. "I told you on the phone, and I mean it, if there is any favor you want from me, just ask."

I thought for a moment. "You know, having been raised by a single mom who worked her tail off for so many years, I have always wanted to give her a once-in-a-lifetime experience. A memory she would forever cherish."

"I like the sound of that," he said. "So what are you thinking?"

"I'd love to have her take a flight on Air Force One if that's even possible."

"Well, Tim, you know, buddy"—President Trump offered a thoughtful nod—"I love ya. Let's make it happen."

A little over a year passed, and with all the drama that followed the president, the constant barrage of attacks from the media, and the continuous onslaught from my colleagues on the Left, I figured he had long forgotten his offer, and I had no plans to bring it up again.

But I was wrong. I soon received a call from the president's secretary, asking if my mother and I would like to join him on Air Force One. He was flying out to a football game and said he had a couple of extra tickets.

"Mom, are you working tomorrow?" I asked on the phone. I was in my office in DC and my mom was at home in South Carolina.

"I am. Why? Do you need something?"

"I need you to take a day off at the hospital and join me in DC. I'll book your flight. I've got a surprise for you."

My mom still worked full-time at Bon Secours St. Francis Hospital. She had been there for more than forty-five years. Though she could have retired years ago, she loved her work and always told me, "It keeps me young."

"What do I need to wear to this surprise?" she asked.

"Wear something comfortable. Nothing too fancy," I said.

I kept the mystery going as we drove to Joint Base Andrews. But as we parked and began walking toward Air Force One, my mother grabbed my hand and stopped dead in her tracks.

"That's Air Force One!" she said breathlessly.

"It sure is." I smiled. "Tonight, you and I are guests of the president of the United States."

Mom's eyebrows shot up as she looked at me with both wonder and fury. "Wear something comfortable?" she said in an unbelieving tone as she smacked my chest with the back of her hand. "Nothing fancy?"

I felt chastised. I'd been thinking about watching a ball game, not who we were watching it with. "Mom, you look amazing. Now come on, we don't want them to leave without us."

As we walked onto Air Force One, her eyes and her smile were as wide as I have ever seen them. Someone from the president's press team asked who was joining us, and I introduced her.

"This is my mother, Frances Scott," I said.

Mom was so beside herself that she had to shake the hand of everyone on the plane. Over the next few minutes, she introduced herself to numerous staff and members of Congress.

When we made our way past the curtain to where the president and his team were sitting, I didn't think Mom could have been more thrilled. I was wrong. She saw President Trump talking with his chief of staff and gripped my hand.

"Timmy, that's the president," she said. "He's sitting right there."

"Yes, Mom, that is the president. Who else did you think was going to be here?"

Before Mom could respond, President Trump spotted us. He stood and made his way over, extending both his arms wide. "Oh, my goodness. You must be Tim's mom. I'm so glad you're here," he said as he gave her a hug. "It was such short notice, and I honestly wasn't sure you'd be able to make it."

"Well, yes. No. Of course. Yes," Mom said. "We wouldn't miss it for the world."

She became even more flustered when President Trump walked her over to where he had been sitting and pulled out his chair. "Please, have a seat."

"Oh, no. I couldn't possibly sit in your chair," Mom said, disbelieving.

"Today, Frances, you are my guest of honor, and this is your chair." He waited. Mom had no choice but to sit.

President Trump offered her a drink before he sat down beside her. For the entire flight, he treated her like a queen. He asked her questions about her life and shared some of his own memories. At one point, they were both laughing so hard that you would have thought they were the best of friends with a long history stretching back many years.

———

On June 16, 2015, when Donald J. Trump came down the escalator and announced he was running for the office of the president of the United States of America, the media went crazy. Late-night talk shows and comedians had found their material for the next five months. It was as if no one else were running. Half the pundits thought it was a business stunt by a man who recognized the benefits of publicity and had no desire to serve as president. The rest just thought he was a joke.

Back then, there were very few people in Congress or around the country—on either side of the aisle—who thought Trump had a chance. In short, all the "experts" in the United States of America knew exactly what was going to happen. One of the establishment candidates would get the nod, and Washington, DC, would continue as usual.

But many of you could see what was actually happening. An enormous number of American women and men knew in their heart of hearts that Donald J. Trump didn't just have a chance, he was the long-sought answer to what they had been looking for. He was someone who saw them as people whose voices needed to be heard. He recognized their inherent worth in a way no one else in Washington was willing to do. They would be no longer forgotten or ignored.

I fully understand that what I have just shared is going to set some people's hair on fire. But it doesn't make the statements any less true. A large portion of this country have not just *felt* forgotten for a very long time; they *have been* forgotten. The "flyover" states, as some politicians and newscasters disrespectfully call the noncoastal states, are the rural and agricultural centers of our nation, and they are as much a part of our great nation as the large urban metropolises with significant electoral votes. But it has been generations since they have been treated as equals.

I honestly don't think it was the baser parts of President Trump's personality that inspired the enthusiasm that resulted in his election. People were attracted to him because he admitted out loud that he didn't care about political norms. He was willing to be brazen in the pursuit of his aims, even if it was not acceptable to the establishment. Contemporary society may not have thought there was still a place for the John Waynes of this world, but apparently there remains a desire for strong, decisive—perhaps even unconventional—leadership.

Big media has spent decades profiting from stories of division, hatred, and fear. They would have us believe that every Trump voter symbolizes the worst our country has to offer. They posit that if you voted for President Trump, you are a racist, a narcissist, a Bible-thumping, small-minded bigot—and that is if they are being generous.

By their definition, I am a racist, a narcissist, a Bible-thumping, small-minded bigot. Humankind, however, cannot be boiled down into caricatures, cartoons, or parodies. Every man, woman, and child in our nation bears the image of our Creator.

As I have written throughout this book, my primary driving forces are hope, opportunity, and redemption. I refuse to see the world through any other lens. I refuse to see *you* through any other lens. I believe every person in this country is on a journey of redemption.

The men and women who voted for President Trump voted for a man who *saw* them. The men and women who voted for President Trump voted for a man who *heard* them. The men and women who voted for President Trump voted for a man who *valued* them. It's that simple.

Hope and redemption. There is but one way forward for *all*

of us. We are not as divided as we have been told. Believe it or not, I think this is what drew people to President Trump. This is what still draws people to him. I think he is a man who believes he can fix things.

TWELVE

OPPORTUNITY

2017

We live in a time of unparalleled polarization. People are either 100 percent for something or someone or 100 percent against them. Even a whiff of disloyalty is grounds for being "canceled." While it is true that Republicans are the ones most pushing back against cancel culture, we have our own version of it.

One example is the relationship between President Trump and many of his supporters. Trump supporters are the most loyal in politics. If anyone speaks an ill word toward the former president, they should expect to be attacked. I learned this personally in August 2017.

This was the month of the infamous rally in Charlottesville, Virginia. The rally was officially known as "Unite the Right," but rather than attracting a group of reasonable individuals spanning the spectrum of conservative principles, this gathering was attended by self-identified neo-Confederates, neo-fascists, white nationalists, neo-Nazis, and Klansmen. The rally featured undeniably racist chants, anti-Semitic slogans, and Nazi and neo-Nazi symbols. One of the organizers' stated goals included unifying the American white nationalist movement.

That these groups exist is an undisputed *and* inexcusable fact. But they shouldn't command a moment of our attention. These racist groups do not have and should not have any real foothold in our country. I write about them now purely to paint the picture of how the media can take a narrative and spin it however they want to spin it.

Racist people will always exist. It is impossible to rid the world of every scrap of bigotry. Yet, as I have written many times, we are in the midst of an incredible journey. Only one or two generations back, these kinds of groups were numerically strong and carried an enormous amount of authority. Just one generation ago, these groups had representation in the highest echelons of our government. Between 1909 and 1944, Ellison DuRant "Cotton Ed" Smith was a senator from my home state of South Carolina. He was widely known for his virulently racist ideology and segregationist views and openly advocated white supremacy. I currently occupy the chair to which he once laid claim.

Today, these supremacist groups are scorned. They are marginalized at best. They have no place in our society. My personal strategy is to give them no airtime. But sadly, their voices continue to be amplified by those who seek controversy over content. Our twenty-four-hour news cycle has evolved toward a singular goal: generating viewership. And, in the case of the rally in Charlottesville, they did their job well. News bureaus across the board were more than happy to spread fear and outrage for ratings. They attempted to extrapolate the images of those loud and sometimes violent hate groups into a false portrayal of what America truly looks like.

What should have been a sparse gathering turned into a horrific event. In response to the racist rally, another group, whipped into a frenzy by the media, arrived to put a stop to things. I have no problem with protests. I respect the men and women who showed up to counter these dangerous idealogues. But I believe the whole thing never should have happened.

It didn't take long for the rally and counter-rally to turn violent. Somewhere in the midst of things, a self-identified white supremacist rammed his car into a crowd of counterprotesters, killing thirty-two-year-old Heather Heyer and injuring thirty-five others.

———

Later that day, when I heard the exchange between a reporter and President Trump, I was concerned to say the least. His conjecture that "there were fine people on both sides" bothered me. Let me be clear. I'm not saying every counterprotester was a saint. But it is inexcusable to give even a single word of praise to any self-identified white supremacist.

At the time, I felt an urgent need to lend my voice to the conversation. As the lone black Republican in the Senate, I wanted the president to clarify things. A day or so after President Trump made the statement, I was asked about it during an interview on HBO's *Vice News Tonight* and then again on CBS's *Face the Nation*.

"I believe the president has compromised his moral authority to lead," I said. "As we look to the future, it's going to be very difficult for this president to lead if, in fact, his moral authority remains compromised. What the president should do before he says something is to sit down and become better acquainted, have a personal connection to the painful history of racism and bigotry of this country. It would be fantastic if he sat down with a group of folks who endured the pain of the sixties . . . the humiliation of the fifties and the sixties. This would be an opportunity for him to become better educated and acquainted with the looping history of so many folks, from John Lewis to my mother and so many others, who have gone through the painful parts of the history of this country."

President Trump's ardent supporters immediately attacked me. My Twitter account blew up with people calling me a traitor, a turncoat, and worse. I was reminded by many that just a day earlier the president had categorically and clearly called out the groups—which was true. But in my mind, his comments the following day erased what he'd said before.

I felt it was important to say something because an entire country heard those words, perhaps even took comfort in those words, and those words were simply wrong. I've always believed there are moments in life when you must speak out. I knew it was dangerous to take on President Trump. I often tell people, if it isn't absolutely necessary, don't do it. But for me, this was a moment of absolute necessity.

Not long after my interview on CBS aired, my phone rang. "Hello."

"Senator Scott, President Trump would love to have a chat with you to talk about your interview yesterday."

I knew what I was up against. But I also knew I needed to stand my ground. "Of course," I said. "Let's set it up. I'm looking forward to it."

I hung up the phone with that feeling you get in your chest when you know things are about to get rough. I turned to Jennifer DeCasper, my chief of staff, who was with me. "So I was thinking you and I should hang out with the president tomorrow. What do you say?"

"Oh, crap," she said with a grimace.

I'm not afraid of confrontation. I have no problem standing up for what I believe. But, like the rest of the world, I had watched how President Trump dealt with anyone who spoke against him. Like a true fighter, the president is a counterpuncher. He doesn't always attack first, but once he feels he's been hit, he won't leave the fight until the whole world knows he won.

"Any regrets?" Jennifer asked.

"Not one," I said. "What about you? Do you wish I'd stayed quiet?"

"Not for a second," she said. "But you do realize the entire country is going to have impossible expectations for this meeting, right?"

"What do you mean?"

"Everyone will think you are going to walk in there and change everything about how the president talks about race."

"I'm not worried about that," I said. "Assuming I get a chance to talk, I'm just going to tell him about my experiences. It's hard to argue with experience."

One thing you need to know about Jennifer is that on a normal day she is one of the biggest jokesters I know. But when things get tense, she becomes even funnier.

The eight-minute car ride to the White House took a very long eight minutes. Things were most definitely tense. Unsure whether President Trump was in attack mode and, if so, what that meant for the coming weeks and months, I lost myself in contemplating every scenario I could imagine.

"Listen, Tim, I've got a great 'in' at Dulles Airport," Jennifer said. "I'd be happy to put in a good word for you."

"What?" It took me a minute to process Jennifer's words.

"I'm just saying, I reworked my résumé last night and sent it off to my old boss at the airport. We are clearly a few minutes away from being fired. Anyway, I'm more than happy to see if I can get you a position with me at Dulles if you're interested."

I laughed as the tension broke. "That depends, would I still be your boss?"

"Oh, most definitely not," she quipped. "You don't have any experience. But I think, with a little time and effort, I might be able to get you promoted to baggage sorter."

The exchange continued until we reached the White House. Both of us exited the car feeling far more relaxed than we had when the drive began.

———

The walk into the White House and down the hallway was a little surreal. Every person we passed stopped what they were doing to watch us walk by. I could feel the expectation in their eyes. I didn't know what it meant, but every person we passed clearly had feelings about the upcoming meeting.

"Why is everyone staring?" I whispered as we walked.

"You must have something in your teeth," Jennifer whispered back.

Part of Jennifer's job is to worry about me and how I come across in certain situations. Did I come out a winner? Did I look like I was afraid of confrontation? Did I live up to the expectations of my constituents? What damage could come from this meeting?

But much to her chagrin, I never cared about any of these questions. I just want to do my job to the best of my ability. If my poll numbers are favorable at the end, great. But even if they are not, character has always been more of a driver for me than optics.

As we entered the Oval Office, I had the fleeting observation that this was my first time in this storied room. Unfortunately, rather than taking the time to truly appreciate the experience, I was trying to process the importance of my presence in that moment.

President Trump rose and walked toward us with a big smile. He seemed almost jovial as he greeted us. Already inside the Oval Office was Vice President Mike Pence as well as Chief of Staff John Kelly. *He brought his A Team*, I thought as we all greeted each other before taking our seats.

This isn't a "wag your finger moment"; this is an olive branch moment. As that thought solidified, President Trump leaned in.

"Okay, Tim. I saw your interview yesterday. You and I don't see that situation the same. I really want to hear what you have to say."

For a moment I was shocked. This was the last thing I expected. "Well, Mr. President . . ."

For the next twenty minutes or so I told President Trump the stories of my grandaddy and my mother. I told him stories of things I had faced in my childhood. While I painted a picture of our collective journey, I also spoke of the way many people like to pretend the journey is already complete.

"There are so many people of color, young and old, who are hurting, who have spent their entire lives without ever feeling valued or even seen. While we have come so far as a nation," I said, "any comment that could even be slightly construed as positive toward white supremacists is just wrong."

For those twenty minutes President Trump didn't say a word. He just listened.

"There are a whole lot of people out there who heard what you said and were wounded by it," I told him.

It is hard to explain the emotion in the room. But everyone was leaning in, seeming to take in every word.

"Okay," President Trump said. "So tell me how to help those I have offended. How do I help the people who are hurting?"

Again, I was stunned. This was not at all going as I expected. I glanced at Jennifer with a raised eyebrow. She offered a small smile and nodded in agreement. Without hesitation, I launched into an idea I'd been trying to get traction on for years. "Well, Mr. President, I believe I do have at least part of the solution . . ."

I began to paint the picture of a plan I'd been dreaming of that would bring serious private investment into lower-income neighborhoods. "Today, Mr. President, private businesses have no incentive to rebuild blighted communities. But I have a plan that would bring resources back into the poorest areas of the country. These are disproportionately minority areas . . ."

I proceeded to tell him about what I had dubbed "opportunity zones." While the president had listened intently the entire time, he became excited when our conversation came to the subject of rebuilding communities. President Trump has always been a builder, and without realizing it, I was speaking his language.

"Tim, I understand incentives better than anyone. Listen, I'm a dealmaker. It's what I'm great at. I think this idea doesn't just help one group; it moves the economy of the entire nation forward. Right? This is what we need. Something that creates success in America."

"Yes, sir," I said, getting excited as well. "People are always talking about the United States being the land of opportunity, but for me the biggest question has always been: Are those opportunities available for every American no matter where they live? And I don't believe they are, Mr. President."

"Okay," he said. "Explain."

"I had friends growing up who were brilliant. And I don't mean just smart; they were hard workers. These guys could really hustle. But a few of them ended up selling drugs or making bad choices, not because they were bad kids, but because the only clear opportunities in front of them weren't good."

"Sure." President Trump raised a skeptical eyebrow. "But I've heard a little of your story. You made it out. You obviously found the right opportunities."

"I did, yes sir. But I had a praying mother, loving grandparents, and mentors who poured into my life. Not every kid is so blessed. When there are no businesses in your neighborhood, where do you apply for a job? When there are no restaurants nearby, what drives people to visit your neighborhood and spend money there? If there are no people coming to your neighborhood, there is no reason for businesses to invest. Without investment, there is little community engagement. It's a vicious cycle that leads to greater disparity with each passing generation. We need to create a reason for the builders, for the Donald Trumps of the world, to invest in neighborhoods like the one I grew up in. This is the only way to bring opportunities to the people who live there. The more private investment we can steer into the poorest zip codes, the better the outcome will be for our nation."

"I love this! I do, Tim! Let's get this done," he said as he stood and excitedly extended his hand. "Let's make things grow and make them better! Our country needs to be better about these kinds of things."

I left the White House with my head spinning. I'd been pushing at the idea of opportunity zones for years and hadn't found even the slightest bit of traction. The next day, I was stunned to read about President Trump answering a question as he boarded Air Force One. When asked about how our meeting went, he started talking about the importance of rebuilding lower-income neighborhoods through opportunity zones.

———

From that day forward, I was able to utilize the power of the president of the United States and his influence to make opportunity zones a reality. It came to fruition through the 2017 tax reform bill. To date, more than $75 billion of private equity has been committed to these neighborhoods throughout the country, and that number is ever expanding. This is one of the things I am most proud of, and it would not have been possible without the aid of President Trump.

While speaking out against President Trump was uncomfortable, to say the least, had I remained silent, I most likely would still be pursuing a Herculean effort of advocating for opportunity zones with no success. Instead, the progress is real. I can walk you through a large swath of downtown Charleston, South Carolina; Erie, Pennsylvania; Atlanta; Baltimore; and numerous other major cities and rural regions across our nation that continue to be transformed thanks to opportunity zones.

From the day of our meeting in the Oval Office up to now, President Trump and I have had a good working relationship. On occasions when I didn't vote as he had wanted, he called me.

"Tim," he said, "I see you voted against me on this one."

"Yes, Mr. President, I sure did."

"Well, you were wrong. But maybe we'll see eye to eye the next time around."

My positive experiences with President Trump weren't purely on a personal level. I clearly remember the hour or so I spent with the president and Attorney General William Barr where no cameras or reporters were present. We were meeting with a large number of families who had lost a loved one at the hands of the police. The only purpose of this meeting was to offer the family members the opportunity to share their stories and advocate for their communities. When the meeting started, the tension and distrust in the room was palpable.

"Thank you all for being here," President Trump said, opening the meeting. "I know this is not an easy conversation to have, but I truly want to hear the stories you came to share."

One by one, each of the family members began to share vastly differing stories of losing a loved one. Every few minutes President Trump would offer a probing question or words of sincere sympathy. As the meeting progressed, because of the graciousness of President Trump, the tension in the room subsided. He listened carefully and was attentive to the pain and the misery of the families.

A relative of Botham Jean was also in the room. When she shared her story, President Trump was clearly angry at the injustice of it all. At the end of the meeting, he turned to Attorney General Barr and asked him to look into a couple of the cases. Not long after, and as a direct result of the meeting, President Trump signed an executive order stating that co-responders should endeavor to bring a mental health expert to a scene whenever necessary.[7]

Don't get me wrong. I have had plenty of moments during the Trump candidacy and presidency that were hard. There were plenty of moments when I had to do a double take. The "s***hole countries" comment grieved and angered me to my core.[8] It didn't just affect international relations; it was demeaning and belittling to entire nations. When the president took a shot at the city of Baltimore, calling it "a disgusting, rat and rodent infested mess" to compare it to what was happening with illegal immigrants at the border, I absolutely felt the need to speak out.[9]

I could continue with a number of anecdotes about the language and some missteps made by the former president. But I also believe he is a fighter. What is even more important to me is that he fought for this nation. I am very proud of all we accomplished. But they were a difficult four years. Though I truly wish at times he weren't so abrasive, I also believe he did the best he could for our country.

Rather than bemoan or try to soften the harsher edges of the president, I found it was best to learn to utilize them. I think the reason President Trump didn't come out swinging in our first Oval Office meeting is because my criticism was founded on something real, something personal. I think he appreciates being challenged, so long as the challenge is about real issues and the challenger is offering a solution, or, if not a solution, a glimpse through a window the president may never have peered through before.

While I understand a large portion of America was offended by President Trump and his leadership style, I also think he was pushing back against an impossible onslaught that began the first day he stepped into the office.

Shortly after President Trump was elected in November 2016, there was an article in the *Washington Post* reporting that efforts were already underway to impeach him.[10] Before he ever stepped foot into the White House, many of my colleagues on the other side of the aisle were already trying to get rid of him. And that played out every day for the next four years. I don't know how that would wear on me, but I imagine it wouldn't wear well.

I began this chapter expounding on the narrative that's being pushed on us daily. We see it on the news and read it in social media. It's a narrative our children are being taught in schools. We are told we are a racist, divided nation. That we have not progressed since the days of our founding. That we have never worn the white hat but instead have always played the role of the villain, the oppressor. And that there can be no redemption for a nation founded on slavery.

First and foremost, the idea that there can never be redemption is an all-out lie. The idea of an impossible ending is the very nature of redemption.

If you believe the narrative being spun, you can't stay positive. Cynicism and negativism are the dominant forces of our news. Bad news sells, and we have figured out how to package it and send it around the world with the click of a button. I am convinced that half the rage against President Trump was manufactured. Every day he was turned into a caricature, a cartoon villain.

I know the man, and I can tell you firsthand how much he cares about this country. I say this knowing that even a single supportive comment will cause some to work themselves into a froth of rage.

We are all imperfect. We are all flawed. And if you are standing on a global platform, your flaws are amplified. But I believe everyone is redeemable.

When I am offended by someone, I choose to confront them. I choose to fight for what I believe until my dying breath, but I don't need to tear someone down in order to win. I encourage you to do the same. Turn off the news channels and step away from your social media for a few weeks. Then watch as your anger dissipates. That very simple choice will make you feel a whole lot better about the world.

Even in a world bent on dragging us down, we must remain determined to see the bright side of life. It's there, waiting for us on the other side of our cynicism.

THIRTEEN

HONOR THE BLUE

2014

It was impossible for Brian to sit inside a Chick-fil-A without experiencing a lifetime of emotions. As he opened the box of his amazingly tasty grilled chicken sandwich, he paused for a moment, closed his eyes, and let the memories wash over him.

Brian's father, John Moniz, had operated a Chick-fil-A until the day he passed away. Brian's earliest memories were of busing tables and taking out trash every Saturday when his dad brought him to work. After a few hours of helping, his dad would give him and his brother four or five dollars each to spend at the arcade in Northwoods Mall.

Brian was thirteen when his father died. John had always been Brian's hero, and the shine hadn't worn a bit all these years later. Brian knew his father was watching from heaven, and he was going to make his daddy proud.

For as long as he could remember, Brian had wanted to be a police officer. Even as a boy he'd always had a very protective personality. The idea of wearing the blue, of keeping his community safe, felt like the perfect fit for him. After high school, Brian took a number of courses on criminal justice and couldn't wait to apply to the police academy. The problem came when he asked his high school sweetheart, Selene, to marry him.

"I will only marry you if you don't become a police officer," she said. "I will not go to bed every night afraid you might not make it home."

In the end, love won out, and Brian gave up his dream to serve and protect. Instead, he entered the family business and began operating a Chick-fil-A in Myrtle Beach, South Carolina. For the next fifteen years, he tried to achieve the same kind of success his father had before he died. John had won the first-ever Chick-fil-A "Symbol of Success" award, which was given for beating a previous year's sales record by 22 percent or more. John was also the first to receive a brand-new Lincoln Continental, which was given to the manager with the best sales record each year.

All these years later, Brian had met and surpassed all his goals, and he was allowed to pick any Ford he wanted. He chose a Ford F-150 4x4 Crew Cab. He loved that truck as much as his daddy loved his Lincoln.

For the last three or four years, however, Brian told Selene he wanted a new challenge. He didn't know what that challenge was exactly. He just needed something new, something that would inspire him. It certainly wasn't law enforcement, though. Policing wasn't even on his mind at this point. That dream was long gone.

One morning, Selene said something that left him speechless. "Fifteen years ago, I told you I wouldn't marry you if you became a cop. I've always felt a little guilty about that, and I'm sorry. I think you should try it if you really want to."

Brian was stunned. He was forty years old. *Was it even a possibility at forty?* he wondered. Slightly worried Selene might change her mind, the next morning Brian drove to a police station and applied.

A year or so later, he was sitting inside a Chick-fil-A with his brothers and sisters in blue, grabbing a quick dinner before his shift. As expected, Brian loved being a police officer. That might even be an understatement. Brian felt fulfilled in a way he had never imagined.

It wasn't lost on Brian that he was the person asked to step into the most intense moments of people's lives. You don't call the police when things are going well; you call them when you are afraid, hurt, or in trouble. You call them when you have no other options. With every call, Brian understood it was a huge honor to step into the lives of absolute strangers and do what he could to help. The fact that he played an important role in keeping his city safe made him feel fully alive.

That night, before he took the first bite of his sandwich, a call came in from the walkie-talkie clipped to his belt. "Ten triple nine. Repeat, ten triple nine in the vicinity of Folly Road south of Wappoo Creek Bridge."

Before the dispatch ended, Brian and his comrades had dropped their meals and were out the door, leaving their chairs and table upended. Ten triple nine is the code for "officer down."

Unsure exactly where to go, Brian headed toward West Ashley. As he drove, the address came over his radio, as did an announcement. "Be advised," the dispatcher said, "there is an active shooter at the scene."

As he drove, Brian retrieved his cell phone and called Selene. "Hey, baby," she answered.

"Selene, listen to me. I'm driving toward an active shooting and there is an officer down. I just wanted to tell you I love you, and I may not be able to talk for a bit. I will call you when I can."

Only silence answered him.

"Selene, did you hear me?"

"Yes. Yes. I heard you. Brian . . . make it home."

"Yes, ma'am," he said. "I love you."

"I love you too."

Brian hung up the phone and turned a corner. A half mile up the road, the Wappoo Creek drawbridge was raised to allow a boat to pass beneath. There were no cars waiting at the bridge, so for a brief moment, Brian thought about jumping the span. The drawbridge is not big, and a car could most likely make it across. Thankfully, he didn't have to decide. Whoever was working the bridge that night must have heard the sirens because the bridge slammed down, and Brian and the two squad cars behind him screamed across it.

As they pulled into the apartment complex, two squad cars were already there with lights flashing. Brian quickly assessed the situation. Three officers were on the stairs, and one was standing on the second floor, aiming her pistol at a nearby apartment. The apartment door was riddled with bullet holes, and someone was lying motionless at the foot of the door.

Rat, tat, tat, tat, tat, tat, tat, tat, tat!

A spray of bullets exploded through the door. Someone inside was shooting at the officer at the top of the stairs.

Still inside his squad car, Brian ducked. *That's an assault rifle!* He hit the gas, tires squealing as he drove to the side of the building. Shutting off the ignition, he reached back and pressed the button to release a shotgun. He could have chosen a rifle, but the shotgun was the first thing his hand touched, and he knew every second mattered.

Rat, tat, tat, tat, tat, tat!

Bang! Bang!

Rat, tat, tat!

Bang!

The sounds of the assault rifle rang again. This time someone was firing back. Brian's colleagues climbed out of their cars, and together they ran toward the center stairwell of the building. As they approached, two deputies descended the stairs, carrying another officer who had been shot in the leg. Brian glanced at him as they passed. *He'll live.* The wound didn't look serious, thank God.

As they began to ascend the stairway, a fourth deputy, who was hunched near the top of the stair with his pistol gripped tight, threw his hand out toward them, motioning for them to stop.

"Go back around to the other side," he said in a harsh whisper as he motioned toward the stairwell at the far side of the building.

The apartment building was two floors with an open-air hallway. It boasted a metal railing and a stairwell in the middle and at each end. Brian didn't hesitate. He leaped from the stairs, darted past his fellow officers, and sprinted to the stairwell at the far end. As he neared the top, he slowed and crouched down for the final few steps.

Ever so slowly, he lifted his head to survey the scene. Brian's breath caught. Immediately his eyes landed on an officer sprawled on his back in front of the apartment door riddled with bullet holes. The officer lay unmoving in a widening pool of blood.

Brian tore his eyes away from the scene and ducked back down, pressing his back against the wall. For a brief moment, he squeezed his eyes shut. *Please, God. Please! No!*

Brian opened his eyes to see his fellow officers looking at him with concern.

"What is it? What did you see?"

Taking a deep breath, he handed the officer his shotgun. *It's time to go to work* was the only thought that flashed through his mind.

Rising ever so slowly, he crouched low, creeping as quietly as he knew how. It was when he was maybe eight or ten feet away that he stopped, suddenly feeling dizzy. He knew the officer lying in the pool of blood. Just a few hours earlier the two of them had been laughing together and "cheers-ing" with multicolored Oreos.

Each month, the department held an informal party to celebrate one of the deputies on a particular squad who did a noteworthy job the month before. It was their fun version of being named employee of the month. You were chosen by your sergeant because you had done something outstanding. Rather than a plaque with your name on it, the department had something far more enticing. At each gathering, every officer was expected to bring a different kind of Oreo. The more exotic kind you could find, the better. At the party, everyone exchanged Oreos and offered a "cheers" to the outstanding officer. That very night, Deputy Sheriff Joseph John Matuskovic had won the award for deputy of the month.

As Brian made himself move forward, he had a stray thought: *I can't remember why Joe won this month. I just remember it was something amazing.* Brian dropped to his belly and crawled beneath the window and over to Joe.

"I got you, buddy. Just hang tight," he whispered into Joe's bloody ear.

Joe was not a small man. If Brian had to guess, he was probably 250 pounds. For a brief moment, Brian tried to lift Joe and carry him over his shoulder. But between trying to stay low and silent and the fact that he was still recovering from a torn hamstring, it simply wasn't working. Instead, Brian began to pull Joe across the concrete walkway toward the top of the stairs. As he dragged his friend, Joe's wounds became clear. He'd been struck in the head, in his duty belt, and in the hip.

Brian blinked away tears, trying not to look at the thick trail of blood. As he dragged his friend, he heard a grunt. To this day, he is unsure whether the grunt came from him or Joe.

"I've got you, buddy. It's going to be okay. I've got you."

Tears escaped from his eyes as he neared the top of the stairs. Lifting Joe to a sitting position, Brian tried to get underneath him to place Joe on his shoulder so he could walk him down the stairwell. Standing at an awkward angle, Brian quickly realized his already torn hamstring wasn't going to let this happen. Collapsing on top of his friend, Brian gritted his teeth and began pulling Joe down the concrete stairs.

When he reached the bottom, he dragged Joe around the side of the building and laid him on the ground.

"Officer down and unresponsive," he gasped into his radio. "I need EMS. I need someone here right now."

"That's a negative," the response came. "This is still an active-shooter situation. They're not coming. You are going to have to bring him out."

Anger and desperation shot through him. "Look, I've got him down the stairs. I'm on the side of the building. I need you to send EMS!"

"Once again, that's a negative. They're not coming. You're going to have to bring him out."

Brian knelt beside Joe, placing his hands beneath his friend's bloody shoulders, getting ready to lift him. Just then, another deputy came up and dropped a bag beside him.

"I brought the med kit," he said. "You need to start working on him."

Brian's hands shook as he retrieved the kit. There was so much blood. *Where do I even begin?* Suddenly, Brian noticed the red flashing lights. He turned to see EMS arrive on the scene. They had disregarded the orders to stay away. An officer was down, and they were putting their lives at risk to save him.

As the medics began to work on Joe, doing everything in their power to save him, Brian and the other deputies stood guard over their friend.

SO THEY CALLED THE POLICE

Brian told me recently that when he thinks about that day, he probably already knew Joe was dead, but he'd been unable to process it in the moment.

Joe Matuskovic died on September 8, 2014, in the line of duty.[11] He was responding to a call that a man was walking around the apartment complex pounding on people's doors and threatening them, and also smearing feces on their doorknobs and windows.

The people in the apartment complex were afraid, and they didn't know what to do. So they called the police. When Deputy Matuskovic arrived, he saw the man run into an apartment. He knocked on the door, and a spray of bullets answered him. There was no warning.

I know Brian Moniz. We grew up together. I've already written about the first time we met. He was the little pip-squeak who used to come into the movie theater with his younger brother, Philip, who became a deputy sheriff in Charleston County. Brian's father, John Moniz, was my mentor who operated the Chick-fil-A in the mall where I worked.

When Brian told me this story, he wept through it. He had

nightmares for months. While I have a number of close friends, Brian and I have been like brothers for as long as I can remember. When I first ran for Congress, it was Brian and Selene who walked the entire city and put up signs and knocked on doors. Their two incredible children, Peyton and Ella Rae, call me Uncle Tim. And unlike some hateful people who use the term in a derogatory way, when they say it, it warms my heart.

In the first five months of 2021, when I am writing this book, thirty-seven officers have been murdered. That's not counting the officers who've died in the line of duty facing countless other inherent dangers of the job. Many have been killed in car accidents in pursuit of a subject or drowned during an attempted rescue. Scores of officers died from COVID-19 because, of course, law enforcement, along with other frontline workers and responders, kept going to work every day despite the pandemic.

2015

LET'S DO SOME GOOD

Kassy could never have imagined exhaustion would feel so good. This morning, it had been her turn to attend the 4:00 a.m. dance party. Her six-month-old son, Sal, seemed to think 4:00 a.m. every morning was the perfect time for such an event.

Her husband, Greg, awakened at 5:30 a.m. to spend some time with his son before leaving for work, giving Kassy one last hour of glorious sleep. At 6:30 a.m., Greg carried Sal back into the bedroom and laid him on the bed next to her.

"Sorry, babe," he whispered, "I have to go to work." He bent low and kissed Kassy on the forehead before disappearing out the door.

Kassy rolled over to see Sal grinning at her. "What do you say we reschedule tomorrow morning's meeting for a couple of hours later," she said.

Sal made a cooing noise.

"Yeah. I didn't think so." Kassy reached out and tickled Sal under the chin. He began to babble, the incoherent yet very communicative language of a six-month-old.

Kassy dressed for her morning run and stepped outside. It was a crisp, clear day. The sky was blue, and the first signs of fall were showing on the trees. As she buckled Sal into the stroller, she thought through her day. Having a six-month-old while trying to finish her doctorate in psychology meant she had to take full advantage of every minute of naptime.

As Kassy stepped out the front door with the stroller, Greg was nearing the precinct. Today was his first day as a field training officer. This meant he was the guy who taught the new recruits the ropes. He'd had a couple of opportunities to move up to a higher position, but he'd turned them down. He loved being a street cop. The idea that he was serving his community and keeping his city safe made him feel great. Adding the privilege of serving as a teacher and mentor to the next generation of officers made going to work that much better.

Around 7:30 a.m., a call came through on the radio. "We've got a suspicious person reported in the parking lot of the Richland Mall."

Turning to the young recruit beside him, Greg grinned. "Okay," he said, "let's go do some good." He turned the vehicle around and drove to the mall. When they arrived, they were the second squad car on the scene. After speaking with the other officer, Greg learned a bank teller had made the call.

"She's seen the same panel van outside the bank for a number of days," the officer told him as he pointed toward a windowless van a short distance away. "She called because she said this morning there was a man sitting inside, watching the bank for a very long time. Understandably, she was a little nervous."

As the three officers approached the van, Kassy was returning home. She put a sleeping Sal down for a nap, took a quick post-run shower, and immediately resumed her work on her dissertation.

That's when the first call came in. "Did you hear about the officer-involved shooting at Richland Mall?" a friend asked. "I just wanted to make sure Greg was okay."

Kassy hung up the phone not really feeling all that nervous. She had been married to a police officer for seven years, and she had learned to wait. The job is dangerous, and Greg had been involved in a number of challenging situations, as he called them. He was a good cop, a great cop. He knew how to carry himself, and he knew how to stay safe.

As more friends texted her, Sal awoke from his nap. It was far too early for him to wake up, especially after the dance party, so Kassy sat in the rocking chair, trying to get him back to sleep. As she did, she began reading news articles on her cell phone. There had indeed been a shooting at the mall just down the street from where they lived.

A few minutes later, a knock came at the door. Suddenly Kassy froze. In that moment, the knock told her everything she needed to know. She carefully placed a sleeping Sal back in his crib and walked to the door. She felt as if the world were moving in slow motion. Standing at her doorstep was a female officer. Directly behind her was the chief. A few steps farther back was the sheriff.

There was no greeting. Just an apology. "I'm so sorry, Kassy," the chief said, "but he's gone."

Kassy suddenly felt as if she were floating outside her body.

Looking down at the gathering from above, she saw herself. She watched as Kassy Alia broke into a million pieces.

—————

When Gregory Thomas Alia approached the man in the van, the man became agitated and confrontational. When he ran, Greg pursued. When Greg tackled him, a short struggle ensued, and the man pulled out a forty-caliber handgun and shot Greg in the head, killing him instantly.[12]

I never had the honor of meeting Greg Alia. The first time I spoke to Kassy was on the phone shortly after her husband had been murdered. I called her to ask if there was anything I could do to help.

"Yes," she said, "please continue to stand up for the police all across this country."

I promised I would, and I have done my best to keep that promise. Kassy and I have since become friends, and she's shown me a strength that I could only hope to have.

"Tim," she once confided in me, "there's such a divisive narrative out there that I am afraid people won't understand what was lost. Greg always knew it could end like this. He went out every day, making an active choice to sacrifice his safety for the good of his community. But I am afraid his death will amount to nothing more than a tally for one team versus the other."

Kassy talks a lot about the us-versus-them, the-police-versus-the-community narrative. It is a pervasive narrative. But it isn't true. As I've said countless times already in this book, the media rarely covers the real story. They cherry-pick sensationalized moments from across the nation and use them to craft a salacious story that will drive viewership, increase clicks, and sell ads.

They reach back to the admittedly shameful origins of the earliest organized policing to paint today's officers and the communities they serve as racist and unjust. Conflating the two is tantamount to comparing a tin can telephone to the internet.

The real story isn't as easy. I believe the vast majority of men and women in blue are upstanding citizens who deserve our respect. Police and community are meant to work together for a better world. And for the vast majority of police and community interactions, this is the way things are. There is no us-versus-them. We are all part of one shared human family. Our joy, our pain, our losses are all connected. Unfortunately, unity doesn't sell on the nightly news.

The brutal and unnecessary deaths of Trayvon Martin (2012), Walter Scott (2015), George Floyd (2020), Daunte Wright (2021), and many others must not be ignored. Their stories should be told so that we not only honor their legacies but show the world that we are a just nation. We hold people accountable no matter what their job, their race, their income level, or their title. We should know and say their names. And we do.

But what about the names of Joseph John Matuskovic and Gregory Thomas Alia? I would argue their names should also be known.

The best way to honor the legacies of *all* these individuals is to prevent senseless murders from occurring in the first place. And believe me when I say, police and justice reform have been priorities for me long before these issues became political flashpoints.

The truth is, police reform is fluid; it's always happening. As training and technology get better, so too our heroes in blue. Over the years, I have spoken with hundreds of men and women in blue. Not one of them is against the idea of better training and more accountability. Every single officer I have spoken to would love to have more intensive training on de-escalation, which means everyone goes home alive. It means Greg would be celebrating Sal's graduation. It means Joe could participate in more Oreo ceremonies. It means Trayvon, Daunte, George, and Walter would be celebrating birthdays, taking vacations, or watching Netflix.

I have said over and over that only the best should wear the badge. We owe it to our communities and our nation to start with the best-caliber candidates and provide them with the training and resources they need to do their jobs. And we must hold them accountable when they don't.

I grew up in the neighborhoods that Brian Moniz now protects. I can tell you firsthand what my community thinks of Brian and his brothers and sisters in blue. When my mom came home from work at midnight, she was grateful when she saw a police cruiser parked nearby. When my family and I came home to find our house had been burglarized, we were relieved there was someone to call who came to help us put our lives back together.

But policing is a thankless job. Not only that, the women and men who are risking their lives to protect us and our property are demonized, their characters impugned. Is it any wonder far fewer men and women are applying for the job?

———

Over time, Kassy was able to forgive the man who murdered her husband. When I asked her how she found the strength to do it, she told me, "I'm a mother. When I look at my son, all I want is the best for him. Then one day I realized that the man who murdered my husband had a mother too. And she probably had big dreams for her son. But at some point in his life, he must have fallen on hard times. I just wish someone would have stepped in and offered help. If that had happened, Greg would still be here today."

After Greg's death, Kassy founded Serve and Connect, a nonprofit organization that works with law enforcement and communities to "improve neighborhoods challenged by poverty, crime, and neglect by building trust, optimizing collaboration, and fostering a shared sense of pride."[13] Kassy turned the most horrific experience of her life into something beautiful. Her son will know the seed of love is stronger than the seed of bitterness.

It is people like Kassy through whom the narrative of redemption flows. Turning personal tragedy into societal gain is what will drive our nation forward. This is the story of America I believe in.

FOURTEEN

JANUARY 6

2021

You might think I'd be embarrassed to tell you the amount of time it took me to pick out my socks each morning, or to admit that on one particular day I had spent nearly thirty minutes searching for and ordering the perfect pair of standout socks. But a gauntlet had been thrown down, and I have never competed for anything with second place in mind.

The challenge had started with a simple comment I made two months earlier. "I thought we had a dress code up in here," I'd said with a grin.

"Senator?" Eugene Goodman, Capitol Police officer, quirked an eyebrow.

I pointed to his socks. They were spectacular. Striped in myriad colors with some form of animal I couldn't quite make out. Was that a meerkat?

Eugene didn't miss a beat. "Article two of the Capitol Police uniform code clearly states that 'no on-duty member shall wear any article of clothing visible to the public containing language of a social, economic, or political nature that might be considered as an advocacy statement, or that might create controversy.'"

My jaw dropped before I could stop it.

Eugene grinned widely. "As Capitol Police we are trained to be prepared for everything," he said as he pulled up his pant leg to show just how big his personality was. "Besides, if you had socks half as cool as mine, you'd be wearing them too."

What should have been an innocent and easily forgotten exchange became a minor obsession of mine. I did own a few pairs of socks that were *almost* competition caliber, and for a few days they would have to do. The following morning, as I strutted my way into the Capitol, my socks were noteworthy to say the least.

"You inspired me," I said as I lifted a pant leg.

Eugene gave a nod of approval before lifting his own pant leg to show just how far behind I truly was. Stars, moons, suns, bursts of color. The man's socks were magnificent. Noticing my reaction, Eugene patted me on the shoulder. "It takes a strong man to admit defeat. Just how strong are you, Senator Scott?"

This was the moment my obsession began. This was a sport I would compete in. I couldn't wait to get in front of my laptop and start searching.

"Eugene, if I lose, I will happily admit defeat. But this isn't a sprint, it's a marathon," I said. Without another word, I continued walking toward my office, my head held high.

"I see how it is," Eugene called after me. "And I accept your challenge!"

I couldn't help but smile in response.

———

The day-to-day responsibilities of a US senator can easily blur together. I have been either in Congress or the Senate since 2011, and when I look back, I remember plenty of moments, but the weeks, months, and years are indistinguishable from one another.

I love being able to represent my state and this country. It is the greatest honor of my life. At the same time, it can be all-consuming. And it should be! There is plenty we need to fix that's been broken for far too long. In the early years, I thought of my time here as a sprint. I had a twenty-page list of things I wanted to get done, and every item on that list was close to my heart.

As a freshman congressman, I remember feeling humbled and excited to serve. It didn't take long to learn that the job of a congressman was far more consuming than that of a county councilman. South Carolina budgets were measured in billions. When I arrived in Congress, as a country we were spending $3.8 trillion, with hundreds if not thousands of issues to focus on. I also wasn't just a new member of Congress but the first African American Republican from South Carolina elected to the House since 1897. This meant the additional pressure of having to do lots of press to explain who I was and what I stood for. In those early months, every day I felt as if I were drinking from a fire hydrant.

A member who'd been in Congress far longer took me aside one day and told me with a knowing smile, "Tim, it takes a minimum of ten years for something you present to the House to become an actual law—if it ever does. Whatever it is you bring to the table will be studied under a microscope, argued over, and sliced apart until you might not recognize it anymore. And then, in a decade or so, you might see something slightly resembling it come to fruition."

To be honest, this advice irritated me. *I was going to change things!* I thought. All these years later, I still refuse to accept a ten-year timeline, but I have a little better perspective. The process of turning an idea into a law, for the most part, should take time. The vetting process of any new law or bill should be robust. Getting buy-in, while frustrating, should be necessary to the process and can often help to make the bill better.

I'd come to Congress to get things done. I'd promised change to the people of the First District of South Carolina. As a senator, I have traveled to every county in South Carolina multiple times. Regardless of whether you love me, hate me, vote for me or for the other candidate, I represent each and every South Carolinian, no matter their ideology, no matter their income, no matter their race, no matter their religion. I have heard complaints on every issue you can imagine, be it taxes, prison reform, police reform, public roads, infrastructure, lack of indoor plumbing, school choice, elder care, fraud, labor unions—you name it. When I think of these things, I feel a sense of urgency. We need to get more done! These and so many other issues need our attention.

Most new staff members take a few years to realize I don't actually love politics or policy. But I do love the people I represent and the country I am privileged to serve, even if I don't lie awake at night and dream about tax reform. When I do lie awake at night, I see the faces of my constituents. I hear their voices in my head when they tell me they're struggling to make ends meet, let alone pay their taxes. I understand I have been granted the honor of being in a position to help them.

———

One of the reasons I am a US senator today is because of a street I helped to get paved in 2001. Literally. I was on the county council in Charleston, and I helped push through a policy that paved the roads in a community filled with crumbling roads. It might seem like a small thing, but helping this community with a simple paved road had both immediate ramifications and lasting significance for that community.

Probably my biggest driving force came the day my mentor and friend John Moniz died. John had a mantra he lived by.

"Tim," he told me on more than one occasion, "before I die, I want my life to positively impact the lives of one million people."

His words were inspirational. What an impossible and awesome dream! John loved his wife and kids with abandon, but he also loved everyone he met. He sacrificed his time, talent, and treasure investing his life and wealth into his community.

As a nineteen-year-old, I remember getting the call when I was at Presbyterian College. "Tim," Brian said through tears, "my dad's . . . he's gone. He died suddenly last night of a coronary embolism."

The world spun after I hung up the phone. I remember praying for Brian and Philip; their sister, Lauren; and their mother, Janice. I felt a deep urgency, a compelling need to honor John in some way. I closed my eyes, and in that moment, I discovered my mantra, my purpose in life.

Before I die, I prayed, *please let my life positively influence the lives of one billion people.*

To be honest, I didn't really understand how big a million was, let alone a billion. I was nineteen, and it sounded like a big number. I know now it was a ridiculous goal. Impossible! Yet it was this goal that motivated me to become a public servant. And it is what drives me today as I continue to look for ways to meet the needs of even more people.

I go to work every day with the voices of my community in my ears. Communities who need paved roads and good housing, new textbooks and good teachers, nutritious food on the table, and good parents with a job. These are the people whose lives I want to affect!

But I digress. Let's get back to the important issue of socks. Because my days blur together, I try to do little things to create memorable moments. It helps to slow the world down a bit.

Officer Eugene doesn't just have great socks; he has a great personality. I love competition no matter how small it may be. I thrive on it. I can turn virtually anything into a competition if I put my mind to it. I don't need to win—okay, I don't *always* need to win—but I love to compete. When something shifts from a goal to a competition, I suddenly try harder. It's subliminal, but it's real.

The game of "Who has the best socks?" played out for almost three months. I looked forward to these moments with Eugene every morning. Before long, a few other Capitol Police officers had become our judges. On more than one occasion I pointed out how the judges might be biased, but my pleas fell on deaf ears. I'm not saying the game was rigged, I'm simply providing context.

On the morning of January 6, 2021, I honestly can't remember what socks Eugene or I were wearing. While I assume we compared them, I honestly can't remember that either. Other events unfortunately wiped the winner from the history books.

My colleagues and I were gathered inside the Senate chamber for a largely symbolic reason, since the act of certifying an election is basically a procedural process. It's a foregone conclusion, hardly controversial. In our more recent history, in every other presidential election, someone from one party or another has chosen to make the symbolic act of not adding his or her name to the certification. But this act does nothing to change the outcome of the election.

On the afternoon of January 6, 2021, most of the senators were in the chamber. We'd barely started the process when, from inside the Capitol, the sound of protesters suddenly rose far louder than it should have been.

"What do you think is going on out there?" I whispered to a nearby officer.

She was also looking in the direction of the door. "I'm sure it's just the protesters outside," she whispered back with a slightly disbelieving tone. "Let me go take a look."

Maybe a minute later, not only could we hear the shouts of the protesters, but we could feel them. Everything stopped as all eyes turned toward the doors. Seconds later, the officer burst back in, followed by three other officers.

"We're shutting this down. You all need to stay here. The Capitol has been breached, and we don't have any idea how many of them are inside. Hundreds, from what I could see. And we have no way to tell how many of them are armed. Do not leave this room until we can find an escape route," she instructed. Without another word, the officers sprinted out of the chamber.

At that moment, I was more certain than I had ever been in my life that a fight was coming. *If I'm going down, I'm going down swinging*, I told myself. Everything felt heightened as I took off my jacket, loosened my tie, rolled up my sleeves, and grabbed a pen, holding it tightly in my fist. It was the only thing I could find remotely resembling a weapon.

A short while later, the same officer who told us to stay put opened the doors wide. "I need everyone here to follow close and stay quiet."

More than ninety senators and probably almost as many staff members spilled into the corridor. The shouts of the protesters were thunderous.

———

On September 18, 1793, George Washington laid the US Capitol cornerstone at the southeast corner of its foundation. Symbolically, the Capitol was meant to be the nation's most important and architecturally impressive building. The construction of this storied building wasn't completed until 1826.

Over the years, the US Capitol continued to expand and to be updated. But one thing that never changed was the enormous amount of marble used throughout the construction. While undeniably beautiful and structurally remarkable, the marble floors and walls amplify sound exponentially.

The shouts of the people who breached the Capitol in 2021 reverberated in every direction.

The vice president of the United States presides over the Senate, and the Senate honors these individuals with a collection of marble busts and paintings displayed throughout the Capitol. As we were rushed down the corridor, my eyes drifted to the past vice presidents, and I wondered how many of these works of art might be destroyed by the rioters.

Bang!

Everyone stopped for a brief moment as what sounded like gunfire ricocheted down the corridor.

Bang!

A few terrified screams accompanied the sounds of flash grenades.

The current demographic makeup of the Senate is the oldest in

American history. We have numerous members in their seventies and eighties. This meant running at any real pace simply wasn't an option. The elevators had all been shut down. So the only available route was a nearby stairwell. I followed at the back to make sure no one was left behind.

In the basement of the Capitol are tunnels that lead to the three Senate office buildings and four House office buildings. Built into the network of tunnels is a subway system, but that had also been shut down per protocol.

With no other option but to run, we made our way through the tunnels. The only sounds were of our labored breathing and unsteady footsteps. As we ran, my eyes drifted up. Hanging from the tunnel ceiling are the flags of every state. They are hung in the order by which the states joined the Union.

In heightened or dangerous circumstances, I don't tend to panic. Usually, it takes a few days for the reality of the moment to fully sink in. But as we ran away from the Capitol, I was more concerned about my staff and my many colleagues who were too old to keep up the pace for long.

After maybe twenty minutes of running, we reached the Philip A. Hart Senate Office Building. When we arrived, we had no context for what was happening. Unlike the rest of America, we hadn't seen any videos. Our only context was the thunderous shouts of angry rioters and the sounds of gunfire and flash grenades.

The Capitol Police led us to the second floor of the Hart Building and into Room SH-216. The room was a logical choice. It is very large and far easier to defend than the porous Senate chamber. It is also far enough away from the Capitol that, unless you know your way around, you might not find it. I estimate there were ninety or more senators with at least half as many aides crammed into that space by the time we were all inside.

But this room was anything but calm. I was surrounded by friends and colleagues, many of whom had lost their bearings and were growing more anxious by the second. Many of the older senators were seated, attempting to catch their breath.

Directly in front of me, a large group of senators were yelling at one another, angrily shouting each other down as though it were some kind of blaming match. I wanted no part of that, so I kept walking.

After a few more steps, I happened upon another colleague who was staring in blank disbelief. He kept repeating, "The United States Capitol could never be breached! This can't be happening!"

Off to my left, more accusations were being hurled. Two members were using colorful language as one tried to place the blame for what was happening on the other.

I turned and surveyed the room. Panic had set in. People were pointing fingers at one another. And then a senator yelled at the top of his lungs, "Shut up! Just shut up!"

Not far behind them, I saw a friend retrieve a small survival knife from somewhere and hold it in a clenched fist. I suddenly realized I still held the pen I had grabbed earlier, my makeshift weapon.

I dropped the pen and took a deep breath. The thought that kept pounding through my head was, *This is so unproductive.* I walked through the chaos toward the front of the room where a podium and microphone had been set up. "Hey, guys . . . ladies." I checked to see if the mic was on. "Senators!"

Silence came quickly as everyone turned their attention to the podium.

"Look, if you want to point fingers about how the Capitol was breached and why we didn't see this coming, great. There's a time and a place for that. But right now, more than anything, we need to come together. If there is ever a day we need to be unified, it's today. If there is ever a time to show deference to one another, it's now."

I searched the room until I found the man whose words we all needed in that moment. "Chaplain Black, I am grateful for your presence, and I am thankful for the ministry you provide. I think it will be appropriate for you to come pray for us."

Barry C. Black nodded as he met my eyes and made his way to the podium. He has been the Senate chaplain for more than eighteen years. He is a retired two-star general and a man I deeply admire. When I'm in Washington, I attend a weekly Thursday morning Bible study led by Chaplain Black, and we have prayed together more times than I can count. Right then, I felt we needed to hear from him more than anyone else I could think of.

Just a couple of hours earlier, Chaplain Black had opened the day with a short one-line prayer. I still remember his words: "Help our lawmakers to remember that history is a faithful stenographer and so are You, God. Amen."

As he approached the podium, I stepped back.

"Thank You, Father God, for the protection You have already provided us and for the promises that You have given us in Scripture," he began. "They are exceedingly great and precious. The promise in the fifth Psalm, verse twelve states the upright are surrounded with the shield of God's favor. Lord, we are grateful to know we are surrounded by the shield of Your favor. Isaiah 54:17 states that no weapon formed against us will prosper. Lord, You did not say the weapon would not be formed. You did not say the weapon would not come against us. So I am grateful for that promise. Romans 8:28 states that You are working everything for the good of those who love You, who are called for Your purpose. Sovereign God, help us to major in loving and minor in everything else. Amen."

By the end of the prayer, everyone was far more cooperative. The temperature of the room had cooled significantly. Rather than laying blame, we sought a plan. The mob outside was there to ensure we did not do our job. They clearly were willing to resort to violence to stop us from doing the purely symbolic act of certifying the election. It was at that moment that we decided nobody was going home until we had finished the work we'd come to do. We remembered who we were and what we were supposed to accomplish. And nobody was going to stop us.

Soon an officer entered the room to take a quick look. "From what we can tell, the only building breached is the Capitol," he said. "But we are going to keep everyone locked down until we can be sure."

Everyone in the room went silent. It wasn't the officer's words that captured our attention. It was the spattering of blood on his face and on his uniform.

Between Chaplain Black's prayer and a collective understanding that America's best were risking their lives to keep us safe, our perspective shifted. Over the next few minutes, Room 216 of the Hart Building became a fortress as armed-to-the-teeth Capitol Police and National Guards were posted at every door.

During the wait, most of us reached out to our staff, trying to make sure they were in a safe place.

———

I don't care who you voted for or what you think about the 2020 election—what happened on January 6 was wrong. It was a sad day for our country. Destruction of property, breaking and entering, threatening officers and officials with kidnapping and murder, attacking officers, even death—this is the reality of what happened that day.

While I believe a number of people need to see the inside of a jail cell for what they did, in the same breath, I don't think every person who entered the US Capitol had mayhem in mind. I believe a large number of them came late and, for the most part, never realized just how violent things had been.

It's been said that the collective IQ of a mob drops nearly fifty points. It is clear to me this phenomenon happened on that day. I am often asked who I hold responsible for what happened. I think this is an odd question. It's as though people want me to blame an ideology or a party or an individual. I hold the people who perpetrated violence, destroyed property, and threatened lives responsible. People are responsible for their actions and behavior, and they should pay accordingly. Regardless of ideology, we are all ultimately responsible for our own actions. And I believe this tragic day was the culmination of individuals making bad choices.

Over the following days, like the rest of America, I watched the video of Capitol officer Eugene Goodman leading the mob away from the Senate chamber. Like the rest of you, my breath caught as I watched his courage play out before this angry mob. Though I wasn't surprised by it, it was still powerful to see.

Now that the chaos is over and life has gotten back to normal, when I happen to catch a clip of that day and see Officer Goodman, my eyes drift to his feet, hoping to catch a glimpse of his outstanding socks. Feel free to watch the video and pause it every few seconds. I have. Unfortunately, his socks never make an appearance.

I believe Officer Goodman deserves every accolade he's been

given. I also believe, while outstanding, he is not an outlier. Most of us will never be asked to face down and outwit an angry mob. Yet every day, countless citizens of this country perform small acts of courage. Every day, men, women, and even children choose to become the answer to someone's prayers.

Officer Goodman did not pick or choose whom to rescue because of his ideology. He did not place blame or accusation against anyone. His job was to protect the Capitol and its occupants, and that's exactly what he did. I wonder if he knows that by protecting the Capitol, he protected what America stands for.

We are a nation of people who put the needs of others above our own. We are a people who love with abandon. Most heroes will never be filmed, and most acts of love will be seen only by those we help and by our Creator. But those deeds of generous, selfless love make us who we are.

FIFTEEN

THIS LITTLE LIGHT

1863

Amos Humiston's eyes were glued on the town below. Thirty, maybe forty fires sent thick plumes of smoke billowing as a steady cadence of gunfire echoed across the hilltop.

"You ever going to take a bite, or do you just plan on holding the food near your mouth and hope it jumps in?" Mark, a fellow soldier, said with a forced grin. To emphasize his words, he shoved a spoonful of boiled, salted pork into his mouth and chewed hungrily.

Amos tore his eyes away from the town. *I am hungry*, he thought as he offered Mark a half smile and took a bite.

"You think we're going to be asked to go down there?" Mark asked, his grin dissolving into a look of fear, his eyes suddenly haunted.

"I don't know," Amos replied as his eyes darted back to the plumes of smoke. "All I know is my feet are killing me."

The two soldiers had endured a series of grueling marches up and down Virginia. The choking dust and blazing heat had taken its toll on the more than four hundred men in the 154th New York Infantry Regiment. Amos let his eyes drift to the surrounding hills and toward Rock Creek. The sheer number of men was hard to comprehend. Tens of thousands were camped, stretching as far as he could see. Never in all his life had he imagined so many people in one place. And that was just on the Union side.

Accompanying the gunfire from the town below were the constant screams of the dying. Amos looked at the faces of the men in his regiment. *How many of us will still be standing by the end of the day?* he wondered. A full 40 percent of the 154th had been lost at the Battle of Chancellorsville two months earlier.

Amos slid his finger over the scar on his chest. He'd been struck by a spent bullet during that battle. It had hit him in a rib just above his heart, and every night when he lay his head down to sleep, he relived the experience in his dreams.

Amos finished his last bite with regret. The salted pork and sparse spattering of vegetables were barely enough to sustain a child, let alone a grown man. *If we don't die in the field, we may just starve to death.* Fighting off the dark thoughts, he wrapped his hand with a tattered cloth and grabbed the pot of boiling water from the fire. Carefully, he poured the fluid down the barrel of his rifle before passing the water over to Mark. As Amos continued to clean and load his rifle, his mind drifted to home.

Amos fished out an ambrotype—an early kind of photograph. He struggled to hold back the emotions stirring inside his chest. Philinda, his wife of nine years, had sent it to him a month or so back, and it was without a doubt his most prized possession. He placed his fingers over the serious little round faces staring back at him: eight-year-old Franklin, six-year-old Alice, and four-year-old Frederick ("Freddie").

"All right, men," Lt. Col. Daniel B. Allen called out as he emerged from the command tent a short distance away. "We've got our orders. Most of the Eleventh Corps are pinned down. We are heading to the northeastern outskirts of the town to cover their retreat."

For just a moment no one moved. The men simply stared at their lieutenant.

"Men, I know you're tired. But this is what we do. This is why we came all this way. Our brothers are down there, and they need our help." Lt. Allen clapped his hands. "Are you with me?"

Amos stood. "Yes, sir," he shouted, offering a salute. "We're with you!"

One by one the men shouted their assent as they stood and retrieved their cartridge boxes and rifles.

Over the next half hour, the 154th made their way down Cemetery Hill and into the town. The closer they came, the louder the sound of fighting became. Soon screams seemed to be coming from every direction. Scores of homes had been set aflame, filling the air with dark smoke. Amos and the rest of the men coughed as they tried to cover their mouths with hands or elbows.

The ground was littered with bodies. On the other side of town, a battle was raging. Amos and his brothers-in-arms double-timed it toward the screaming and the gunfire and soon reached an area known as the brickyard. They formed a battle line at a split-rail fence just below the crest of a ridge. Before Lt. Allen could give any kind of order, disaster struck. Two Confederate brigades attacked, seemingly from out of nowhere. Amos and his regiment were outnumbered more than three to one. They didn't have a chance.

Thirty-three-year-old Sgt. Amos Humiston was shot through the hip and leg, but he ran as fast and as far as he could. He made it about a quarter of a mile before succumbing to his wounds. As Amos lay dying in a secluded spot at the corner of York and Stratton Streets in Gettysburg, he retrieved his ambrotype. *I'm sorry*, the thought formed slowly. *I love you, my little ones. God be with you.* Fixing his eyes on his children, Amos Humiston breathed his last breath.[14]

Over three days at Gettysburg, the Union Army of the Potomac suffered more than 23,000 casualties, and Confederate casualties totaled more than 28,000. Though the Civil War would continue for almost two more years, it is the Battle of Gettysburg that turned the tide of the war for the North.

It is estimated that 618,222 soldiers died during the Civil War. Of that number, 360,222 Union men gave their lives to atone for our nation's "original sin," and 258,000 Confederate soldiers were killed.[15] This is by far the greatest toll of any war in American history.

When Amos Humiston's body was found, he was propped up against a wall. His eyes were still open and staring at the photo of his children clutched in his stiff hands. There was nothing in his pockets to give anyone a clue as to who he was. Everyone from his regiment was either dead or nowhere to be found. The only identifying thing he owned was the ambrotype of his children.

When you have the time, look up the story of the photograph held by Sgt. Humiston.[16] Not only does Amos exemplify the bravery of our men and women in uniform—volunteering to protect, to defend, and to serve—his story provides yet another example of everyday Americans going out of their way to improve the lives of people they've never met. These kinds of stories have been playing out since the days of our founding.

Amos's wife, Philinda, and children lived in Portville, New York—a full 242 miles from Gettysburg, Pennsylvania.

Remember, this was 1863. There were more than three thousand dead Union soldiers at Gettysburg alone.

On October 29, 1863, Philinda responded to a notice in the *Philadelphia Inquirer* that published a description of the photograph and asked for help in identifying the unknown soldier at Gettysburg. Her letter was received in early November, and a Philadelphia religious journal, *The American Presbyterian*, published the news on November 19, the very day President Abraham Lincoln gave the Gettysburg Address.[17]

On that day, President Lincoln said 272 words that helped shift the mindset of the nation. In the last bit of his speech, he said,

> It is rather for us to be here dedicated to the great task remaining before us—that from these honored dead we take increased devotion to that cause for which they gave the last full measure of devotion—that we here highly resolve that these dead shall not have died in vain, that this nation under God shall have a new birth of freedom, and that government of the people, by the people, for the people shall not perish from the earth.[18]

I am writing a good bit about the history of race in our nation. The Civil War is a powerful story woven into the tapestry of America. I've heard it argued in recent days that Lincoln's great sin is that he "didn't go far enough." And, because of this, some have even tried to cancel Abraham Lincoln, if you can believe it. While I truly believe everyone is entitled to their opinion—as my pastor tells me, "We all have the right to be wrong"—this is a bridge too far.

In 1865, when the Civil War finally ended, the United States had been torn to shreds. To push the nation even a step further toward complete equality before the law might well have broken us. The very idea that we survived a civil war of this magnitude was already astounding. The following few years were spent actively choosing to forgive and to rebuild, and in doing so, ushering in redemption.

————

When I look at the world today, I think perhaps the single greatest comparison in modern history, at least for me, is what happened in the aftermath of the Mother Emanuel AME Church massacre. In chapter 9, I have already referred to the horrific event during which a man walked into a church and executed nine black Christians simply because of the color of their skin.

Over the following weeks, I had attended nine funerals. While each gathering reinforced the tragedy experienced by individual families and our collective community, it was the funeral of Pastor Clementa C. Pinckney that nearly broke me. Pastor Clementa and I had been friends for almost fifteen years. My uncle had attended his church for more than fifty years. Whenever I visit, I feel as if the members of Mother Emanuel are my extended family. Pastor Clementa was the first person to ever call me "senator." The morning of the massacre, he and I had been texting. I still have the text on my phone. I look at it whenever I miss my friend.

In the aftermath of the mass murder, all of Charleston held its breath, the state of South Carolina held its breath, America held its breath. Would there be riots? Would there be violence and looting? The wound was deep, and the pain and the anger were acute. In that moment, though I would never have condoned it, I fully understood the urge for retribution, the need, dare I say, to claim an eye for an eye. Surely, in this situation it would have been justified.

Just two days later, a representative of every one of the

Emanuel Nine was given the opportunity to address the shooter directly. All of America watched with bated breath as, one by one, each family member not only forgave the murderer but also spoke words of grace and love. These survivors told the killer about the love of Jesus and how redemption was available even to him.

Each was clearly broken. Each wept as they spoke. But rather than say words of anger or hatred, they spoke the language of purest love. These men and women were concerned for the heart and soul of the man who had just murdered their pastor and their loved ones in cold blood.

These powerful people understood the truth that forgiveness is as much, if not more, for the forgiver as it is for the forgiven. Holding on to anger or hatred, holding on to rage or pain, will eventually destroy even the purest of heart. Forgiveness doesn't just offer redemption to the one who hurt you; it ushers freedom into your own heart.

When most of the world thinks about the story of the Mother Emanuel shooting, they remember the murders. But I choose to remember the blinding light of forgiveness that exploded across our nation. This was the light of freedom, the light of restoration and redemption. How these families responded didn't just shift the identity of Charleston; it altered the identity of our nation.

We are a nation that doesn't simply believe in the story of redemption but also understands our role in bringing it about. This is precisely the kind of healing and forgiveness President Lincoln preached.

———

The generation of Abraham Lincoln and Amos Humiston played their role in our collective story of redemption perfectly. The idea that in one generation they should have stomped out every last shred of racism embedded in our nation's systems does a disservice to their incredible accomplishments. They set the stage for generations to come. They teed up the ball and primed the pump to allow us to rise, to become the heroes who could continue to fight for justice.

The miracle that was Abraham Lincoln and the Civil War shifted the identity of this nation. Our country went to war with itself, fighting and bleeding to forestall injustice. Addressing the greatest sin of our nation head-on nearly broke us. Yet we persisted. It was a miracle, pure and simple. Every last person in this country needs to understand the magnitude of our story.

When the Civil War ended, Lincoln could have cowed the South. He could have berated, belittled, and begrudged the fact that we had to go to war to preserve the Union and to free the enslaved. Instead, he set the South free from their sin. He knew the story of redemption is not about walking away; it's about being made whole again.

David Brooks at the *New York Times* said of Lincoln's second inaugural address:

> This is a speech of great moral humility. Slavery, Lincoln says, was not a Southern institution, it was an *American* institution, weaving through our common history for 250 years. The scourge of war, which purges this sin, falls on both sides.[19]

And he was correct.

The Civil War wasn't "good" Northern states fighting "bad" Southern states. Anyone who looks at history with clear eyes knows some states in the North held slaves. There were simply far fewer enslaved people in the North, at least partly for practical reasons. The Civil War was America fighting for its very soul, for its identity. It eventually came down to two sides, but the struggle was internal.

President Lincoln could clearly see the dangers of half the country feeling a sense of superiority, feeling as if they had gotten it right while others were still struggling. He understood the only way forward was the way of forgiveness, mercy, and love. The only way for America to be made whole again was for us to reconcile our differences and move forward together.

In his second inaugural address, President Lincoln said, "With malice toward none; with charity for all; with firmness in the right, as God gives us to see the right, let us strive on to finish the work we are in; to bind up the nation's wounds; . . . to do all which may achieve and cherish a just, and a lasting peace, among ourselves, and with all nations."[20]

We have deep divisions in our nation. But look at our history. We will fight for what we believe in. We will fight to the death if we must. We will drag our entire country to the brink of disaster so long as we are fighting for what is true and right. And then, when the battle is over, we will forgive. We will embrace. And we will move forward.

The story of Abraham Lincoln and the Civil War is astonishing on every level. Did he go far enough? He went past the breaking point. America was unconscious. The referee was pounding the mat. The three count was milliseconds away. And Abraham Lincoln didn't blink. In the very last moments, he pulled an impossible move, just like my wrestling hero Bobo Brazil, and turned the tables on his opponent.

The stage was set for the next generation to rise. The gauntlet had been thrown. Our history asks, "We were willing to give everything we have—even our very lives—to fight injustice. What are you going to do with the gift we gave you?"

In the aftermath of the Mother Emanuel shootings, our country answered this question by again choosing restoration over separation. May we be brave *and* bold enough in this generation to play our own role in the ongoing fight against injustice.

SIXTEEN

THE BLACK EXPERIENCE

2022

I am completely proud to be an American. I am proud of the progress we have made. The distance we have traversed over the past 245 years is staggering. How far we have come in the past fifty years, in terms of racial equality and justice, is incredibly encouraging.

While writing this memoir, I've endeavored to take you on a journey with me. I am not simply telling my story. I am telling *our* story. But my chief of staff, Jennifer DeCasper, whom you have already met, took me aside this morning and said something that stopped me in my tracks.

"Tim," she said, "I am reading these chapters, and I am loving them. You were such a dork with your buckteeth. I almost felt sorry for you. You were strong on the football field. It was fun to read about your grandaddy and your mom."

"I'm sensing there's a 'but' here," I said.

"But," she said, "I don't feel like I know your story yet of growing up as a young black man in America. And I know you have one. Because, well, like me, you are black. I think you owe it to the readers to not just tell the story of America but to tell them the fullness of your story, which is also the story of being black in America."

I sat back for a moment and pondered her words. She was right, of course. If I don't tell the stories I'm about to share in this chapter, I will not have been frank with you. If you've followed me this far into our story, you deserve to hear all of it. You may love or hate what I have to say, but if I don't say it, then I have painted an incomplete picture.

1987

A night with Grandaddy might not have been considered a hot date, but my girlfriend Eileen and I still had a lot of fun. We had been dating for a few months, and I really wanted her to get to know my family. I wasn't in love just yet, but things were definitely progressing in that direction.

In terms of my overall life at the time, I remember feeling as if I were at the top of my game. My teeth were being fixed with braces, and I was finally driving my own car—a Chevy Chevette. It might not sound like much, but it might as well have been a Mercedes sports coupe to me! I was young and in charge. I felt bulletproof.

It was 10:00 p.m. on a hot Charleston night. I was driving Eileen home after leaving my grandaddy's house. When I turned onto Rivers Avenue, I saw the far-too-familiar flashing lights in my rearview mirror. My eyes flicked down to the odometer. *Thirty-eight in a thirty-five zone. That can't be the reason.*

"You've got to be kidding me," I said irritably as I pulled to the curb. I quickly thought through the past few minutes. I hadn't done anything wrong. *Maybe I have a taillight out?*

"They aren't stopping you for speeding, are they?" Eileen was as confused as I was.

"We'll find out soon enough," I said as I retrieved my license.

We waited in the car for more than five minutes. The officer had pulled us over, but he wasn't exiting his vehicle. I retrieved my insurance papers and wondered why we were just sitting there.

"Why do you think he's not coming?" Eileen asked. "Should you get out and speak to him?"

"I don't think—" I stopped speaking when I saw the officer exit his vehicle. I watched in my side-view mirror as he placed a hand on the holster of his gun and slowly approached the car.

"Here he comes," I said.

I'd been taught by my mother to respect authority. I'd also been taught how to behave when I was pulled over. My hands were locked on the steering wheel and my window was open.

"Son," the officer said, "do you know how fast you were going?" The officer's hand never left his gun.

"Yes, sir." I put on my most apologetic grin. "I think I was at thirty-eight. I know that's a little fast, but I can promise you it was a mistake. I honestly never speed."

The officer bent lower to see Eileen. "Are you all right, ma'am? Do you need anything?"

"Yes, sir. I mean no. I'm just fine. Thank you," she said.

When he turned back to me, he was clearly skeptical. "Can I see your license and registration?"

"Yes, sir," I said as I retrieved them from where I'd just placed them on the dash. This was my mother's second rule. *Have everything ready and waiting, so you don't have to go digging for it in front of the police.*

"Wait here," the officer said as he walked back to his vehicle.

Eileen and I sat in awkward silence as we waited.

When the officer finally gave me back my license, I was feeling so many emotions and I didn't know how to identify any of them.

When we finally were allowed to drive away, neither one of us said a word.

———

The thing about this interaction with the police is that it wasn't anything new. And it wasn't just interactions with police. I have more memories than I can count of people hurrying along to the other side of the road when they see me walking toward them. I have a dozen memories of shopping for a new pair of pants or a shirt with a department store clerk shadowing me the entire time to be sure I wasn't shoplifting. I've been shadowed in grocery stores, if you can believe it. And on more than one occasion.

Just three weeks ago, for the fifth time, I was stopped by a Capitol Police officer on my way into the US Capitol to cast a vote. Each time, after showing the officer my credentials, I was still detained. Each time, I have had to ask my white colleagues to tell the officer who I was.

My brother Ben and I were talking just a few days ago. "Tim," he said, "a man can never fully understand what it's like to give birth."

"Okay, I can agree with that," I said, knowing this was a setup for something to come.

"We can read books about it. We can hear a woman talk about it, painting a picture with intimate details. We can be in the room when our child is born and witness every second of it. But, unless you experience something like that, you can't fully understand."

"I'm tracking," I said. "So where is this going?"

"It's impossible for anyone who didn't live it to understand the pain of growing up black in the South."

If you aren't black, and you read the stories above, I can say with absolute certainty that you cannot understand them. Each of those stories seems relatively small in the grand scheme of life.

Others might say, "Really, Tim? You got followed around a grocery store, and you're complaining about this? Perhaps you need to grow a thicker skin."

"Well, you were speeding after all." I've been told this more times than I care to count. "The police didn't do anything wrong. They just gave you a ticket and let you go. Isn't that their job? What's the big deal?"

These and many other innocent-sounding questions have often come my way.

I have been pulled over twenty-one times in twenty years. On only three or four of those occasions was I actually speeding, and even so, it was never more than five or six miles over the limit. I have been pulled over as a US senator on my way to a vote. I have been stopped as a US senator walking into the Capitol on my way to cast a vote.

So what's the big deal?

I honestly don't know where to begin. Sitting with my girlfriend in my car, I remember feeling deeply embarrassed. No. Embarrassed implies agency on my part, as if I played a role in the scenario. What I experienced that night was humiliation. Cars had been passing me throughout the drive. I was not pulled over for going three miles over the limit. I was pulled over for being black.

Being powerless before someone who is treating you unjustly is humiliating. There's no other word for it. When that person represents the very authority that is meant to keep you safe, it's sure hard to drive away and feel protected by police officers or our justice system.

What I don't think people understand about racism and prejudice is that you don't just experience it in the moment. Rather, it infects your very identity. And when these interactions happen not monthly, not weekly, but daily, each encounter is like ripping open a deep wound that never has enough time to heal.

I don't know a single black man or woman in the South, and probably in the North for that matter, who doesn't wear a scar from such mistreatment. Instead of trying to be more just than those in the system who devalue you, it feels easier to quit. If you think the entire system is stacked against you, and you have experienced proof that it is, why continue forward? Why play any role in a nation that doesn't seem to care about you or others like you?

This is not an easy conversation. A brilliant, heroic police officer can still represent a painful experience to someone who looks like me. Make no mistake. I know intellectually it is not that officer's fault. I don't believe he or she should be held accountable for something they did not do. But having an awareness of the pain and mistrust they can represent to a huge percentage of Americans is more than important. It's imperative.

———

There is the other side of my black experience. As a conservative black man in public office, I experience racism on every level.

Just recently, I was being interviewed on Fox News by my friend Trey Gowdy. He asked me to respond to an accusation that had been hurled at me a day or so earlier. There was nothing new about the accusation. Similar insults have been thrown at me and my party ever since I was first elected as a county councilman. This time the accusation came from Joy Reid on MSNBC.

"You've got to love Tim Scott standing there to provide the patina of diversity," she said, her voice dripping with disdain.

Joy was "reporting" on a press conference I had attended with a colleague who was speaking on the subject of the minimum wage. My colleague was speaking out against a bill that immediately would raise the minimum wage in his state by 50 percent. I have owned and operated a number of small businesses over the years, and I understand how this kind of bill could destroy a small business. This is a subject on which I have decades of experience and about which I have strong convictions.

I care deeply about the communities I represent. You would be hard-pressed to find another senator who has spent as much time as I have strategizing how to bring prosperity to lower-income neighborhoods, and I can tell you that the numbers and the arguments for raising the minimum wage don't add up. I am committed to providing a pathway to success for all Americans, and I know from experience that workers can't benefit from a policy that forces their employers out of business.

Government should be making it easier—not harder—for entrepreneurs to flourish. We need policies that prime the pump of economic growth. It still frustrates me to this day when I think of the volumes of bureaucratic red tape I had to cut through to start my own business. What if the government, instead of standing in the way, cleared the path for the women and men who want to create jobs, invest in their communities, and drive economic growth? This really shouldn't be such a revolutionary thought!

The issues of the minimum wage and the idea of bringing

investments and opportunities into lower-income neighborhoods are subjects I could write about for the next twenty chapters. But I want you to keep reading, so I won't. (But I could!)

I am a black man. I know this because, when I looked in the mirror this morning, I was black. It wasn't a shock. I've been black my whole life. Joy Reid is also black. But I would suggest she has a limited view of the capacity of the people who look like us. In her world, a black man should not be able to have his own opinions about economic policy. And it isn't just her. In the eyes of most liberal elitists, a black man needs to stay in his place, over on their side of the aisle. In their world, the only reason I would ever attend a press conference is to be used as a prop.

I've written a lot about the history of race in this country and how far we have come. Yet there are some who are doing their all-out best to drag us backward. And it is the very people who impugn and admonish us daily, lecturing us about how racist and divided we are as a nation, that are exhibiting these undeniably racist views on national television.

The idea that a black man might know something about the minimum wage or immigration or the economy or international relations or anything at all for that matter should not be a surprise to anyone. Still, whenever I share my (dare I say) expert opinion on these subjects, members of the media and some of my colleagues on the other side of the aisle hurl the same tired, thinly veiled, racist accusations. There is no other way to say it. Their low expectations are the very definition of racism. It's that simple. And I hear it in some way, shape, or form weekly, if not more often.

After I delivered my rebuttal to President Joe Biden's inaugural address, the term "Uncle Tim" started to trend on Twitter. It wasn't cute. It was hateful. They may as well have called me a "house nigger." The idea that having an independent thought is the same as betraying my race is preposterous! If anything, I would argue that refusing to walk in lockstep behind our philosophically liberal president is the antithesis of subservience.

DON'T STAY IN YOUR PLACE

One of the things I am most proud of since coming to Washington is the 2017 tax reform bill I played an integral role in creating. When the bill passed, I was asked to stand beside President Trump at the press conference announcing the victory. Within minutes, actor Andy Ostroy tweeted: "There's *one* black person there and sure enough they have him standing right next to the mic like a manipulated prop."

I quickly responded with a tweet of my own: "Uh, probably because I helped write the bill for the past year, have multiple provisions included, got multiple senators on board over the last week, and have worked on tax reform my entire time in Congress. But if you'd rather just see my skin color, pls feel free."

This started a Twitter storm that I stayed out of. But the hatred and vitriol thrown my way were staggering.

I was standing next to the president because I was one of three senators given the task of wading through the tax code and making changes to it. I worked on the personal side of the tax code, while Pat Toomey (R-PA) worked on the business side and Rob Portman (R-OH) worked on the international side. For several months it was just the three of us.

To be honest, I loved every moment of working on the individual side, in part because it gave me a chance to focus on single mothers. I grew up in a home where there wasn't always enough food on the table, the lights weren't always on, and the phone wasn't always connected. My mom did her best, but we definitely went without some of the basics on multiple occasions. As a result of the tax reform bill, single moms saw their federal taxes cut on average by 70 percent. This made a real difference in the lives of single moms and their families all across the United States.

Yet, to the liberal elitists in the media, I couldn't possibly know anything about business or tax reform. If I was standing in a press conference, it had to be because I was a prop to be pulled out whenever Republicans wanted to look as if they cared about black people. Their response to me simply standing in front of a camera said more about their opinion of black people than anything else.

According to these liberal elitists in the media, the black man or woman better stay in their place and not have an opinion that is not given to them. This is racism pure and simple.

WHAT CAN BRING CHANGE?

The experiences I outlined above needn't define what it is to be black in America. Nowadays, whenever I hear about the "black experience," the only stories I hear are the hard stories. And while I believe these stories are important to tell, which is why I've done just that in this chapter, if you listen to the national narrative, you would think each and every one of us has lived a life of desperate pain, heartache, and misery. You would think black people across our great nation are victims of pretty much everything.

I have had infinitely more positive experiences when it comes to race than negative. My life has not been a life irretrievably marred by racism and bigotry. Today we live in a world that thrives on creating narratives of division. But my childhood and my life have not been defined by my blackness. The vast majority of my life has been defined by family, friends, and mentors who loved me. The majority of my life has been defined by my acceptance of the love of Jesus and the way I choose to view the world—namely, through the twin lenses of hope and redemption.

Oh, my, do I have some of the most brilliant and amazing stories about growing up. These stories shouldn't be told through the lens of race. What a ridiculous way to view the world! But, for the sake of making a point, that is exactly how I will tell them.

Most of my memories, until the age of seven, are about living on an Air Force base. One of the beauties of life on a military base is that whoever shows up is your friend. You don't have black friends or white friends. You don't have segregated housing. From my earliest days, I had great friends of every color.

When I moved in with my grandparents, we moved into an all-black community. I don't know that I understood racism at that point in my life, because everyone looked the same as me.

Later, my middle school football coach would throw my bike in the back of his pickup truck and drive me home from practice, telling jokes and encouraging me. He was white. One of my best friends in the world was Roger Yongue, who taught me the love of Jesus. He was also of a paler complexion.

When I moved up to Stall High School, I shone on the football field and was involved in the student body leadership. This meant I had lots of friends of every color. In fact, during those years, I felt more racism coming from my black friends, who called me "Oreo" on many occasions because I wasn't meeting the expectation of the groupthink within the school.

My mentor, John Moniz, was also white. Al Jenkins is black. Monte Harrington was white. Why am I telling you this? To make a point. All manner of people invested in me throughout my life. Some were black. Some were not. But they all played a role in bringing me to the place I am today.

I don't mean to suggest I am color-blind. The very idea is

impossible, and it also diminishes the beauty of our diverse nation. I believe we must become a people who will celebrate that beauty. We must strive to be a nation that leans into and honors the people who do not look, pray, or sound like us. Our nation is strongest when *all* of America is reflected. This is the hope for our country.

I have spent many chapters telling stories of hope and redemption because that is the journey we are on. I have embraced these truths in the core of my identity. This is who I am. There has been monumental change in our country over the past fifty years in regard to how we see race. Rather than ignore or play down our differences, we have learned to celebrate them. Yet I tell the stories because we must understand not just our collective story but also our individual journeys if we are to move forward together.

I just outlined in the previous chapter the brilliance of President Lincoln. He set the stage for us to go further. And through time and a seemingly impossible journey, step by step, moment by moment, we are continuing his legacy. But we have not arrived. To pretend that we have is wrong. To ignore the wounds our brothers and sisters have borne and still bear—wounds that have attacked their very identity—is wrong. We have a responsibility to better understand those wounds in our society. I encourage you to truly listen to the stories of the men, women, and children who look and believe differently than you do. You have much to learn. Just as I do.

As a nation, we are fighting for our identity. There is no law that will change the hearts of humankind. There is no bill or policy powerful enough to stop racism. So what are we to do? What can bring change? What can we look to that can bring the transformation we need? I'll tell you.

There is hope.

There is love.

There is redemption.

SEVENTEEN

BLIND SPOTS

1951

Ben's earliest memories involved three large buckets, a crank wringer, and a washboard. After a long day of cleaning houses and cooking meals, his mother would arrive home well past dark with two or three sacks of laundry. After she prepared a meal for the two of them, she and seven-year-old Ben would step out to the front porch and begin the lengthy process of washing the clothes of his mother's employers. Ben's mother worked as a maid for a number of people in Charleston.

After brushing the clothes with a bar of soap and scrubbing them along the washboard, his mother would hand Ben the newly cleaned clothes, and he would dunk them into one of the rinse basins. After he had made sure all the soap was thoroughly rinsed off, Ben would then work the wringer. At first, he had enjoyed cranking the handle and watching the clothing slowly be forced through the two spools and the water crushed out of the garments. Yet it didn't take long for Ben to hate the job.

This was a nightly ritual. His mother tried to make it fun by singing songs and telling him stories as they worked. But as time wore on, both of them would inevitably get lost in the rhythms of the work and carry on in silence until every last stitch of clothing was hanging on the wash line.

When Ben was ten, he had saved up enough money to buy his very own shoeshine box. He was as proud of that box as he had ever been of anything in his life. Every day after school, he would run to Spruill Avenue just outside the Navy Yard and set up shop. For ten cents a shine, he would work his brushes and his buffing cloth until he could see his reflection in the shoes of the Navy men.

In 1957, Ben turned thirteen. He was finally old enough to wait with the other young men in the parking lot in Accabee, a neighborhood in what is now North Charleston. Each morning, he would wake up well before sunrise and jog the mile or so to the pickup spot. Before long a bus or truck would stop, and everyone would climb aboard.

For the next ten hours, Ben would work furiously. On his best days, he could pick nearly two hundred pounds of cotton. When the foreman came to weigh the sheets of cotton at the end of the day, more often than not Ben had picked nearly twenty pounds more than many who were twice his age. Though it was back-breaking work, the $1.50 he made for every hundred pounds of cotton was well worth it.

When Ben was fifteen, he saw her for the first time. The girl of his dreams. She was so beautiful that she took his breath away. When she stepped onto the school bus, he immediately stood and extended a hand. "I'm Ben. You can sit with me, if you'd like?"

Ben was in love. He knew in that moment he was going to

marry this girl. The two became fast friends, and they were married by the age of eighteen.

A few years later, in 1963, Ben's life took a dark turn. It was just two weeks after the Birmingham church bombing in Alabama by a group of white supremacists. Ben and a friend, a fellow airman named Terrell, were walking to the local bingo hall on the base where many of the airmen took their wives on dates every Tuesday night.

As they stepped onto Eighteenth Street at the back of the base, five other airmen approached. "Look at the two coons all dressed up in uniforms like real men!" a man sneered.

"Tell me," spat the second. "What are a couple a niggers skulkin' around in the dark for? Don't you know this area ain't meant for you?"

Ben and Terrell stepped back warily. "Listen," Ben said, "we don't want any trouble. We are just heading to the bingo hall."

"You two niggers a couple of queers?" The third man laughed.

"We are going to walk away. We just want—"

Ben ducked as one of the men threw a bottle at him. After the bottle shattered against the wall behind him, the men surged forward in an all-out attack. It was five against two. Even so, Ben and Terrell held their own.

One of the men grabbed Terrell from behind, trying to hold him so he couldn't defend himself. Terrell managed to duck down and spin, punching the man hard in the gut. Ben caught the flash of metal and dove backward as a knife sliced through the air where his face had just been. Then, leaping to his feet, he retrieved the pocketknife he always carried with him.

The man with the knife snarled as he shuffled forward and slashed at Ben, who lurched back and then quickly darted in, slicing a full fifteen inches across the man's belly.

"He cut me!" the man shrieked as his blood spilled onto the dusty ground. "The nigger cut me!"

In that moment, Ben and Terrell knew if they stayed and fought, they wouldn't make it home alive. So they turned and sprinted away in opposite directions.

Stupid! Stupid! Stupid! The thought thundered through Ben's mind as he ran. *Why didn't you just run? Why did you stay and fight?* Terrified, he ran faster than he ever had in his entire life. Barely able to find a breath, he hid in an alley for an hour before he dared come out again.

The man who'd been cut made his way to the hospital. Though the cut to his belly was lengthy, it wasn't deep and required only a few stitches. The man's friends, angry at having lost their prey, actually went back to Eighteenth Street and started fights with a number of other black airmen.

Over the next few weeks, all five men who had started the altercation would be court-martialed for "trying to incite a race riot" on the base.

Ben also went through a court-martial. In those days, it rarely mattered what the provocation was—a black man slicing open the belly of a white man meant prison time. Ben was terrified that he would spend the rest of his life in the federal penitentiary in Leavenworth, Kansas.

By the end of his court-martial, however, justice prevailed, and the incident was ruled as self-defense. Though there was irrevocable proof that he had done nothing wrong, Ben now had a bad reputation with his superiors because of the incident. The stink of the ordeal stayed with him. He was branded a troublemaker, ostracized by his peers, and relegated to the worst jobs on base—all because he had defended himself.

Angry at the injustice, Ben began to drink. It was just a little at first. But as the weeks turned to months, there was rarely a night when he didn't come home having drunk too much.

Two years passed, and Ben was shipped out to Vietnam. It was 1965, and on the day he left, he kissed his wife and two-year-old son goodbye. His wife was six months' pregnant with their second child.

To say Vietnam was a life-altering experience would be the understatement of the century. When Ben returned home 105 days later, besides the unbelievable trauma experienced in the jungles of 'Nam, which he wouldn't speak about for decades to come, he was met at the airport by an angry mob.

"Baby killer!" a young woman shrieked.

"Worse! He's a nigger baby killer!" A young man stepped up to Ben and spat in his face.

Ben stood frozen in the spot, spittle dripping from his chin, watching the young man shout obscenities just inches away. When he finally willed his feet to move, the mob followed, all the while shouting the vilest insults imaginable.

The night he arrived home, Ben didn't say a word to his wife and two kids. He didn't even hold his newborn baby boy. Many hours after everyone was asleep, he wept harder than he had at any point in his life. The enormous amount of pain and confusion boiling inside him was all-consuming.

A full week passed before he spoke a word to anyone. When he finally did speak to his wife, it was with words of anger about the food not being hot enough or the baby crying too much.

The darkness continued as Ben's downward spiral neared a crashing point. He hated being in the cramped apartment with his family. He knew he was letting them down. He knew he needed to be better, to do better, but he simply couldn't find his bearings. The only interactions he had with his wife involved shouting biting and cruel words.

On a snowy day in 1973, Ben truly hit rock bottom. He'd finally done it. He'd gone too far. There was no going back. As he watched his wife angrily throw heaps of their boys' clothes into a suitcase, he could take it no longer.

All the pain and misery of the last few years, the incident with the five airmen and his tour in Vietnam, painted the lens through which he viewed the world. The way Ben saw it, he was a victim who had no choice, no role in the tragedy that was his life. He felt hostile toward the entire world. He was afraid of everything, so he struck out at everyone.

"You are nothing! Do you hear me?" As he shouted the words, he saw the physical effect they had on his wife. Her shoulders caved inward as if she'd been punched in the gut. But it was too late. He knew he couldn't stop her. Frances Ware was far too strong of a woman.

Spittle flew from his lips as he pounded his fist against the wall. "You leave now, and you will regret it for the rest of your life. You are nothing but a coward!"

Frances opened the front door to reveal a thick snowfall, and she hesitated only a moment. Cold wind blew into the apartment as she squared her shoulders and stepped outside to load their belongings into the lime-green Plymouth Cricket.

"I'm not going to let you take my kids away. I will take you to court and make sure you never get to see them again! Do you hear me?"

Frances walked past him without looking him in the eye. "Timmy," she said to her youngest son, "get in the car. We need to leave now."

Her son didn't move a muscle. He just sat there, clinging tightly to his Dallas Cowboys football as if it were the most important thing in the world.

"Timmy, I need you to get up."

"Please, Mom!" Timmy burst into tears. "Please. I don't want to go! Please don't do this!"

Frances glanced at her nine-year-old son, Ben Jr., who sat beside Timmy. He also had tears in his eyes. "Help me with your brother," she said. He stood and placed a hand on Timmy's shoulder.

"Frances!" Ben's shout stopped all three of his family members in their tracks. "Take them away from me and your kids will never succeed. They will be nothing, just like their mama."

Frances didn't turn around. She didn't look back. She merely walked out into the thickening snowfall and climbed into the car.

REDEMPTION WON'T BE STOPPED

Years into my adulthood, I learned that watching us drive away was the worst day of my father's life. On different timelines, through different journeys, all three of us would eventually forgive him. And yet that day is still the moment that will always grieve each of us. Although I saw my dad a few times after, I wouldn't truly reconnect with him until I was in my twenties. And it would be many more years before we established any kind of a healthy relationship.

To be honest, much of what I just wrote in this chapter, I didn't know until recently. I believe deeply that every person is living out a redemption story. I have shied away, however, from learning anything about my father's story. I did forgive him, but then I moved on. The idea of truly reconnecting with him at a meaningful level wasn't something I desired in the slightest. I'd found a way through life without my dad. I didn't receive anything from him as a child or a young man, and I certainly didn't need anything from him as an adult. Or so I believed.

It has been the act of writing this book that made me see my blind spot for what it was. I have written again and again about the importance of not judging someone based on their worst day. But what happens when their worst day is the cause of your deepest pain?

Even so, redemption won't be stopped. The greater the darkness, the more powerful the light. Did you know you can light up an entire dark room with one small candle? Redemption is available for every last one of us, no matter how painful the journey.

Over the years, my father began to pick up the broken pieces of his life and forge them anew. He sought counseling and has left the anger behind. He has now become someone who fully embraces the beauty of what life has to offer.

We all have blind spots, and we all have painful moments we shy away from. Rather than address them with a fist of righteousness, we turn our fists on others. Rather than swallow our pride, we swallow a bottle of vodka. We pretend everything is okay when in reality our world is driving off in a lime-green Plymouth Cricket. If we want to find freedom—true release from life's burdens—we must shine a light on our blind spots.

EIGHTEEN

AMERICA,
A REDEMPTION STORY

By the time this book releases, a major election year will be on the horizon. I want you to envision it with me for a moment. On your social media feeds, during your family get-togethers, when you catch up with friends from way back when—are you going to sow hate or are you going to sow love? When you interact with people who believe differently than you do, how will you treat them?

Elections are vastly important to our nation. Every election has very real repercussions, some of which echo for generations to come. The price of gas, the cleanliness of the environment, the safety of our people—the impact of each election is staggering. Even so, it is relationships, connecting with and loving others, that will change hearts and minds.

I believe every eligible American citizen should vote his or her conscience. Your vote matters! Your vote has the potential to shift the identity of this nation. And, after you have voted, remember that it is the people who love you that matter most. Burning bridges in the name of progress is the opposite of progress.

When President Trump was elected, a very large number of

young people turned on their parents. "How could you vote for a man who . . . ?"

When President Obama was elected, a large number of parents and seniors were offended by their kids and grandkids. "How could you vote for a man who . . . ?"

Such division is one of the saddest things I can imagine.

Diversity is one of the things that set us apart as a nation. We don't only proverbially celebrate each other's differences; we participate in, we embrace, we *love* the differences. We marry people different from us. We adopt them. We hire them. We teach them. Differences make us a better people. Loving your neighbors doesn't mean loving your neighbors because they also put up a Christmas tree and believe in Jesus. Loving your neighbors means the "Hate Has No Home Here" sign or the "Make America Great Again" sign in their yard plays no role in whether or not you say "Good morning, how are you?" and really care about the answer. Love the neighbor who proudly flies the Confederate flag or the LGBTQ flag or the American flag or the BLM flag (or, most especially, the Dallas Cowboys flag).

I challenge you to *become love* in the face of hate. Choose optimism in the face of cynicism. Identify with grace rather than scorn. Step back from your knee-jerk reactions. Let go of your offense and do your best to understand that we are all coming from drastically different places with vastly differing perspectives.

The story of America doesn't belong to a particular group. It is *our* story. And every one of us is given the immense opportunity to add a chapter to that greater story of us. Ours is a story being written even as we breathe. It's a story of love, redemption, mistakes, courage, anger, trial and error, and learning.

Every neighbor, every person you pass on the street, is adding a different flavor to our collective story. Be open to a new chapter. Be willing to be taught a new thing. Be willing to change. You aren't right in all your beliefs, and neither am I. We all have blind spots, and a very large part of growing up is being willing to address them.

When you go to the polls to vote, drown out the noise. Step above the fray and choose to be part of the solution. Then realize that as important as voting is, it is what you do when you leave the voting booth that will strengthen our nation's story.

The federal government can't end racism or stop hatred. As you live out your days, take the blinders off and embrace your responsibility. Stand up to injustice. Love your neighbor. Serve and encourage others. These seemingly small acts take remarkable courage in this climate, and only by exercising our courage can we bring about the redemption we seek.

I don't have to look through the archives of history to find powerful stories of redemption. They are all around me. I am surrounded by friends, family, and colleagues who are currently living out these courageous story lines.

In these pages, I have told the story of my mentor John Moniz, who lived a powerful story of redemption. He loved his wife and raised two boys who grew up to be heroes in their own right. John modeled what a faithful father and husband look like. For a kid like me who grew up without a dad, he showed me what a good father truly was. He played a role in my personal story of redemption.

I told you the story of John's son Brian, who risked his life every day to serve his community. He and his brother, Philip, who is a deputy sheriff in Charleston, are living out stories of redemption.

I told you the story of Al and Robin Jenkins, another couple who played a pivotal role in my story of redemption. They continue to inspire me to this day!

I told you the spectacular story of Madam C. J. Walker, who overcame all obstacles, persevering through the impossible and changing the world simply by refusing to give up.

My grandparents' story is one for the ages. It is a romance filled with every last story bit imaginable. What my grandaddy and grandmama overcame in their lives is staggering.

I told you the story of Monte Harrington, who stepped into my world and became the miracle. What he did for me and my buckteeth changed everything.

I told you the stories of police officers Gregory Thomas Alia and Joseph John Matuskovic. These two men represent hundreds more stories just like theirs that play out every single year. They gave their lives to protect people they had never even met.

I told you the story of Kassy Alia. In the wake of unspeakable tragedy, she found a way to change her narrative and bring beauty to the dark places in her community.

I told you the story of Amos Humiston, a man who volunteered to fight in a war to end slavery. He was a man who loved his family until his dying breath.

I told you the story of Isaac Doctor. His life may have ended in tragedy, but that is not his legacy. His death meant something. His life brought awareness of the sins of our nation. His story traveled far and wide and played a role in moving our nation in the direction of redemption.

I told you the story of Walter Scott. His story, too, is a redemption story; it is not the story of a victim. His life mattered. His death helped bring about real change in policing in South Carolina. His story still plays out today, bringing us one step closer to a truly just society.

I told you the story of the nine saints of Mother Emanuel. The men and woman who lost their lives on that day didn't die in vain. Their lives, what they stood for, what they believed, in echoes today in the lives of their loved ones.

I told you the story of my chief of staff, Jennifer DeCasper. Her story of courage and persistence is one of my all-time favorites!

I told you the story of my father. His is a story of beautiful, mind-blowing redemption.

I told you the story of my mother. Oh, my God, I love that woman. Every day of her life has been a story of a life well lived.

And, through these individual stories, I've told you a story of America. I believe every person in our country is living out a story that could be included in this book. No matter where you are in your journey, yours, too, is or has the potential to be a story of redemption.

Hollywood's greatest writers couldn't dream up a better story than ours. Full of dreamers, overcomers, and unlikely heroes. We could be looking up from rock bottom, or we could be in a season of great beauty, magic, and wonder.

If you are in a place right now where you feel as if all is lost and you can't see a way forward and you're all alone and can't find a shred of meaning, know that redemption is close at hand. Make a decision to get up, to keep moving. Never play the role of victim when the role of hero is waiting for you.

Your story matters more than you can imagine.

IMAGINE WHO WE WILL BE

If you are eighteen when you vote in the 2024 election, you will be sixty-four in 2070. I want you to imagine your life. Your kids will have kids of their own by then. You will be the elder, watching the next two or three generations play *their* roles in paving the way to a brighter future. Our stories will be woven into theirs. They will be our heroes. They will rise. They will be better, do better, love stronger, and accomplish more than we can ever imagine. For they will be standing on our shoulders.

Though it may not feel like it, take my word, 2070 is not nearly as far away as it seems. We will be there before we know it. When you look at the history of our nation through a month-to-month or year-to-year lens, at times it may feel like justice, equality, and redemption are a million miles away. Yet I submit to you that these truths are nearer than you think. I will say it again: we are living a story of redemption, and we are moving swiftly in the right direction.

When you finish this book, I want you to close your eyes and imagine where the world will be in 2070. I am currently living out my grandaddy's dream for this country. By the time he died, he was so very proud to be an American. He is the one who taught me to see the world through the lens of hope and redemption, and he understood our story was still being written.

I can't imagine the next two or three generations without taking a moment to appreciate just how far we've come. It is with this understanding that I view the future. We are a nation of entrepreneurs, innovators, builders, warriors, and pioneers. We are a nation filled with men, women, and children who are fighting for justice and moving the needle through daily acts of love. We are a nation of great diversity, and we're stronger for it.

After you imagine the next thirty or forty years, write your vision down for your grandchildren and great-grandchildren to read. It might feel silly now, but someday they will sit at your feet and revel in the stories of how you played a role in bringing hope and opportunity to your family and justice to our nation.

Most of you I will never meet in person. Even so, I am honored to take this journey alongside you. I am honored to have our stories woven into the greater story of America. Though our lives are but a single thread, together we will weave a beautiful tapestry.

And I, for one, plan to make my story count!

Acknowledgments

I've been blessed in so many ways throughout my life. Yet it has been the act of writing this book that has given me the chance to truly focus on some of the specific blessings. When I think about my life, I am amazed at the myriad friends who have allowed their stories to be woven into mine. There are countless names I could mention, but for the sake of brevity, I will narrow them down to the people who allowed me to tell their stories and who championed me while writing this memoir.

First of all, my mother, Frances, and my aunt (Doretha) Nita Smith. Thank you for all your support and for helping me remember some of the more profound stories of my childhood.

Roger Yongue, Joe McKeown, and Jennifer DeCasper, you have been by my side throughout so much of this journey. Your friendship and expertise mean more than you will ever know. Al Jenkins, I appreciate your wisdom and love our friendship. Thank you for weaving your story into mine. Kassy, Alia, Brian, and John Moniz, thank you for allowing me to tell your stories and for always having my back.

Kevin McCarthy, you believed in me when no one else would.

ACKNOWLEDGMENTS

Thank you for championing me! Trey Gowdy, I am continuously inspired not just by our friendship but by your wisdom.

To my father, writing this book has helped me get to know and love you more, and for that I will always be grateful. Understanding the pain and challenges you overcame helped me understand my story, which inevitably has been influenced by your story.

Joel N. Clark, Angelyn Wollen, Esther Fedorkevich, Daniel Marrs, and the entire team at HarperCollins, it has been an absolute pleasure working with you all. Thank you for your passion and expertise. I am truly grateful.

Notes

1. Walter D. Wintle, "The Man Who Thinks He Can," in *Poems That Live Forever*, comp. Hazel Felleman (Garden City, NY: Doubleday, 1965), 310.
2. See "About Madam C. J. Walker," Madam C. J. Walker (official website), accessed March 25, 2022, https://madamcjwalker.com/about.
3. The three-fifths compromise was an "agreement between delegates from the Northern and the Southern states at the United States Constitutional Convention (1787) that three-fifths of the slave population would be counted for determining direct taxation and representation in the House of Representatives," from Britannica Online, s.v. "Three-fifths compromise," accessed January 25, 2022, https://www.britannica.com/topic/three-fifths-compromise.
4. Anjel Vahratian, et al., "Symptoms of Anxiety or Depressive Disorder and Use of Mental Health Care Among Adults During the COVID-19 Pandemic—United States, August 2020–February 2021," *Morbidity and Mortality Weekly Report* 70, no. 13 (April 2, 2021): 490–94, https://www.cdc.gov/mmwr/volumes/70/wr/mm7013e2.htm; Mélissa Godin, "Survey: Majority of Americans 'Dissatisfied' with State of U.S.," *Time*, July 1, 2020, https://time.com/5862179/pew-survey-americans-dissatisfied-trump-president/.

5. Raychelle Cassada Lohmann, "What's Driving the Rise in Teen Depression?" *U.S. News and World Report*, April 22, 2019, https://health.usnews.com/wellness/for-parents/articles /2019-04-22/teen-depression-is-on-the-rise. See also "Adolescent Mental Health," World Health Organization, November 17, 2021, https://www.who.int/news-room/fact-sheets/detail /adolescent-mental-health.

6. Adam Grant, "There's a Name for the Blah You're Feeling: It's Called Languishing," *New York Times*, April 19, 2021, https:// www.nytimes.com/2021/04/19/well/mind/covid-mental-health -languishing.html.

7. David Jackson and Nicholas Wu, "'Contentious' or 'Compassionate'? Ahmaud Arbery's Relatives, Other Families Meet with Donald Trump to Talk Police Reform," *USA Today*, June 16, 2020, https://www.usatoday.com/story/news/politics /2020/06/16/ahmaud-arberys-relatives-other-families-meet-trump -policing/3197473001/.

8. Joanna Walters, "'Shithole' Remark by Trump Makes Global Headlines—but It Doesn't Quite Translate," *Guardian*, January 13, 2018, https://www.theguardian.com/us-news/2018/ jan/12/trump-shithole-countries-lost-in-translation.

9. Wilborn P. Nobles III, "Trump Calls Baltimore 'Disgusting . . . Rodent Infested Mess,' Rips Rep. Elijah Cummings Over Border Criticism," *Baltimore Sun*, July 27, 2019, https://www .baltimoresun.com/politics/bs-md-pol-cummings-trump -20190727-chty2yovtvfzfcjkeaui7wm5zi-story.html.

10. Matea Gold, "The Campaign to Impeach President Trump Has Begun," *Washington Post*, January 20, 2017, https://www .washingtonpost.com/news/post-politics/wp/2017/01/20/the -campaign-to-impeach-president-trump-has-begun/?postsh are=2711484932964031.

11. Deputy Sheriff Joseph John Matuskovic, Officer Down Memorial Page, September 8, 2014, https://www.odmp.org/officer/22177 -deputy-sheriff-joseph-john-matuskovic.

12. "Police Officer Gregory Thomas Alia," Officer Down Memorial Page, accessed March 21, 2022, https://www.odmp.org/officer /22607-police-officer-gregory-thomas-alia.

13. "Who We Are," Serve and Connect (official website), accessed January 27, 2022, https://serveandconnect.net/who-we-are/ (page discontinued).

14. For more about Amos Humiston, see Ben Fanton, "When Amos Humiston Died at Gettysburg, It Was Only the Start of His Story, One Soldier's Tale," *Buffalo News*, July 4, 1993, https://buffalonews.com/news/when-amos-humiston-died-at-gettysburg-it-was-only-the-start-of-his-story-one/article_26a485b9-e5f8–599b-a574-acbae94ae633.html.

15. William F. Fox, *Regimental Losses in the American Civil War, 1861–1865* (Albany, NY: Albany Publishing Co., 1889); and Thomas Leonard Livermore, *Numbers and Losses in the Civil War in America, 1861–65* (Boston: Houghton, Mifflin and Co., 1909).

16. See, for example, Mark. H. Dunkelman, *Gettysburg's Unknown Soldier: The Life, Death, and Celebrity of Amos Humiston* (Westport, CT: Praeger, 1999).

17. "Wills House Virtual Identity: Philinda and Amos Humiston," National Park Service, accessed January 28, 2022, https://www.nps.gov/gett/learn/historyculture/wills-house-virtual-identity-philinda-and-amos-humiston.htm.

18. Abraham Lincoln, "Gettysburg Address," transcription of the standard text inscribed on the wall of the Lincoln Memorial, Library of Congress, accessed February 25, 2022, https://www.loc.gov/exhibits/gettysburg-address/ext/trans-nicolay-inscribed.html.

19. David Brooks, "America: The Redeemer Nation," *New York Times*, November 23, 2017, https://www.nytimes.com/2017/11/23/opinion/america-the-redeemer-nation.html.

20. Abraham Lincoln, "Second Inaugural Address," 1865, Library of Congress, accessed March 25, 2022, http://hdl.loc.gov/loc.mss/ms000001.mss30189a.4361300.

ABOUT THE AUTHOR

Senator Tim Scott has served in the US Senate since 2013 and brings with him a mission to positively affect the lives of a billion people with the message of hope and opportunity.

An unbridled optimist, Tim believes that despite our current challenges, our nation's brightest days are ahead of us. During his time in office, he has been a tireless advocate for creating more opportunities for families living paycheck to paycheck and helping children mired in poverty gain access to quality education. Tim also knows that in order for our nation to prosper, we must get our spending and national debt under control. He has sponsored balanced budget amendments throughout his time in Congress and will continue working to restore fiscal sanity in Washington.

Tim understands what it means to live at the intersection of hardship and opportunity. He and his brother grew up in a single-parent home in Charleston, South Carolina, with their mother working sixteen-hour days to keep their family afloat. Tim nearly flunked out of his freshman year in high school. But through his mother's prayers, the influence of his mentor, John Moniz, and his own hard work and discipline, he began the process of turning his life around.

The lessons gleaned from his mentor still guide Tim today: you can think your way out of poverty; profits are better than wages; financial independence is a stepping-stone for success; and having a job is a good thing but creating jobs is a better thing.

Prior to public service, Tim built a successful small business of his own. He was first elected to Charleston County Council in 1995, to the South Carolina State House in 2008, and to the US House of Representatives in 2011. In January 2013, Tim was sworn in as a United States Senator from South Carolina, and was re-elected in a special election in 2014 and again to a full term in 2016.

Tim has attended Seacoast Church in Mount Pleasant since 1997.